Sports Illustrated

Sports Illustrated

THE
CANADIENS
CENTURY

INTRODUCTION BY **MICHAEL FARBER**

CONTENTS

Sports Illustrated

PRESENTS

SPORTS ILLUSTRATED GROUP
Editor Terry McDonell **President** Mark Ford
Vice President, Consumer Marketing John Reese

SPORTS ILLUSTRATED PRESENTS
Editor Neil Cohen **Art Director** Craig Gartner
Senior Editors Trisha Blackmar, Kostya Kennedy,
Richard O'Brien **Photo Editor** Jeffrey Weig
Editorial Manager Pamela Ann Roberts
Staff Editor David Sabino **Associate Editor**
Gene Menez **Senior Writer** Michael Farber
Staff Writer Brian Cazeneuve
Associate Art Director Karen Meneghin
Reporters Adam Duerson, Elizabeth McGarr
Associate Photo Editor Kari Stein
Copy Editors Rich Donnelly, Denis Johnston,
Richard McAdams (DEPUTY), Robert G. Dunn,
Jill Jaroff, Kevin Kerr, Anthony Scheitinger,
John M. Shostrom **Special Contributor** E.M. Swift

TIME INC. HOME ENTERTAINMENT
Publisher Richard Fraiman
General Manager Steven Sandonato
Executive Director, Marketing Services Carol Pittard
Director, Retail & Special Sales Tom Mifsud
Director, New Product Development Peter Harper
Assistant Director, Newsstand Marketing
Laura Adam **Assistant Director, Brand Marketing**
Joy Butts **Associate Counsel** Helen Wan
Senior Brand Manager, TWRS/M Holly Oakes
Brand & Licensing Manager Alexandra Bliss
Design & Prepress Manager Anne-Michelle Gallero
Book Production Manager Susan Chodakiewicz
Special Thanks: Glenn Buonocore, Suzanne Janso,
Margaret Hess, Brynn Joyce, Robert Marasco,
Brooke Reger, Mary Sarro-Waite, Ilene Schreider,
Adriana Tierno, Alex Voznesenskiy

© 2009 TIME INC. HOME ENTERTAINMENT.
PUBLISHED BY SPORTS ILLUSTRATED BOOKS.
Time Inc., 1271 Avenue of the Americas, New York, New York 10020.

All rights reserved. No part of this book may be reproduced in any form or
by any electronic or mechanical means, including information storage and
retrieval systems, without permission in writing from the publisher,
except by a reviewer who may quote brief passages in a review.

SPORTS ILLUSTRATED BOOKS IS A REGISTERED TRADEMARK OF TIME INC.
ISBN 10: 1-60320-070-3 • ISBN 13: 978-1-60320-070-7 • Library of
Congress Control Number: 2008909720 • Printed in the U.S.A.

We welcome your comments and suggestions. Please write to us at:
Sports Illustrated Books, Attention: Book Editors, PO Box 11016,
Des Moines, IA 50336-1016. If you would like to order any of
our hardcover Collector's Edition books, please call us at
1-800-327-6388 (Monday through Friday, 7:00 a.m.–8:00 p.m.
or Saturday, 7:00 a.m.–6:00 p.m. central time).

Henri Richard won
11 Stanley Cups, tying
him with Bill Russell for
most team-sport titles
in North America.

COVER PHOTOGRAPH BY DAVID E. KLUTHO;
TITLE PAGE PHOTOGRAPH BY HY PESKIN;
CONTENTS PAGE PHOTOGRAPH BY HEINZ
KLUETMEIER; BACK COVER PHOTOGRAPHS BY IHA/
ICON SMI (5); BRUCE BENNETT STUDIOS/GETTY
IMAGES (3); DAVID E. KLUTHO (3); MANNY MILLAN
(3); BETTMANN/CORBIS (2); FRANK PRAZAK/
HOCKEY HALL OF FAME (2); DAVE SANDFORD/NHLI/
GETTY IMAGES (2); AP; DAN BALIOTTI; JAMES
DRAKE; GRAPHIC ARTISTS/HOCKEY HALL OF FAME;
YALE JOEL/TIME LIFE PICTURES/GETTY IMAGES;
LONG PHOTOGRAPHY; MARVIN E. NEWMAN;
DICK RAPHAEL; ELIOT J. SCHECHTER/NHLI/GETTY
IMAGES; TORONTO STAR/CANADIAN PRESS;
TONY TRIOLO; FRONT FLAP PHOTOGRAPH BY
BETTMANN/CORBIS; BACK FLAP PHOTOGRAPHS
BY FRANK PRAZAK/HOCKEY HALL OF FAME (3);
ARCHIVE PHOTOS/GETTY IMAGES; BETTMANN/
CORBIS; JAMES DRAKE; JOHN IACONO; IHA/ICON
SMI; HEINZ KLUETMEIER; DAVID E. KLUTHO;
JOHN G. ZIMMERMAN

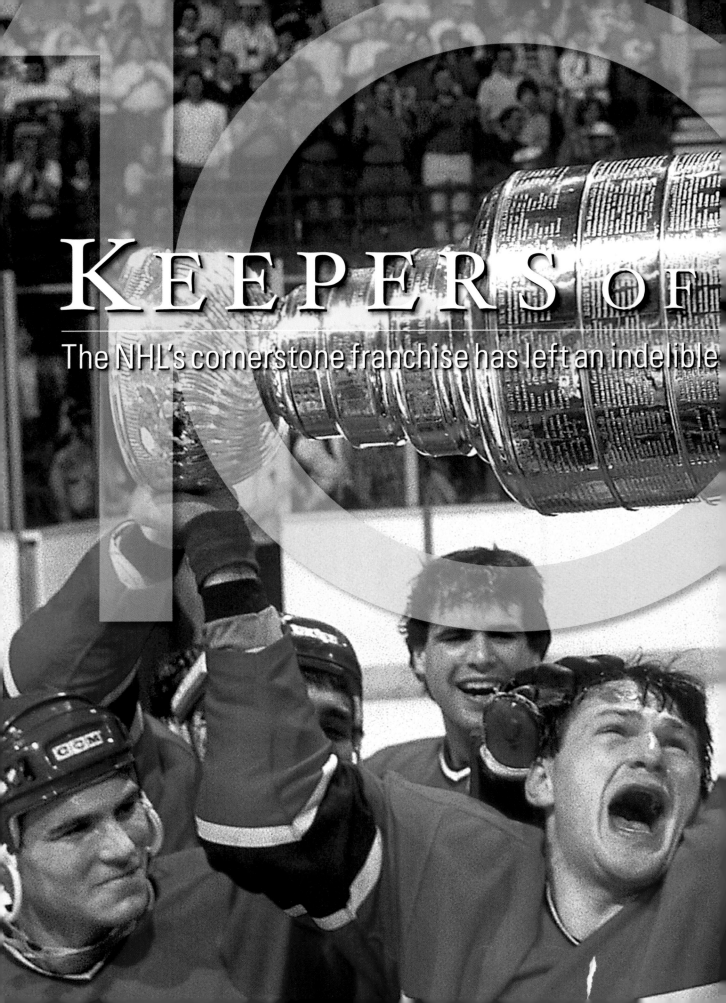

KEEPERS OF

The NHL's cornerstone franchise has left an indelible

THE FLAME

imprint on the game | BY MICHAEL FARBER

Claude Lemieux
(with the '86 Cup) and
Montreal have earned
the right to laud their
history because they
have made some.

FOR MOST BIRTHDAY CELEBRATIONS, A SIMPLE RENDITION OF *HAPPY Birthday* suffices, but this is the 100th of the Montreal Canadiens, who are happiest when they warble a song of themselves. The franchise practically begs for lampooning because of its conspicuous delight in wallowing in its own history—as I am fond of saying, the only two western institutions that really grasp ceremony are the House of Windsor and the Canadiens, but in this momentous season Montreal has found an eager chorus to help carry

its birthday tune. Among the myriad special events the Canadiens have been trotting out since October—vintage-jersey nights, the introduction of a ring of honor and a community outdoor rink at the Bell Centre, the issuing of commemorative stamps and coins, the All-Star festivities—perhaps the most extraordinary will be the

on the Canadiens—in November, Patrick Roy's number 33 became the 15th number to hang from the rafters; if Montreal retires any more, it will have players skating with ampersands and percentage signs on their backs—but they have earned the right to laud their own history because they have actually made some.

  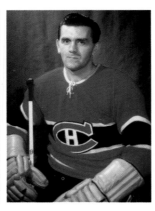

Montreal dominated the league's first 50 years, and Hall of Famers such as Malone (far left)—the NHL's first scoring leader—along with Morenz, Richard and Plante helped shape the game.

April 2 concert at the arena by the Montreal Symphony Orchestra. This time, someone will be tooting the Canadiens' horn for them.

There is old, and there is venerable. Fortunately for the Canadiens, they are both. Old? The Canadiens are as old as the Canadian Football League's Grey Cup, older than income tax in Canada, older than the tradition of American presidents throwing out a ceremonial first pitch, older than the first public performance of Mahler's stupendous *Das Lied von der Erde*. Venerable? Their 24 championships are the most by any North American professional franchise except the New York Yankees. The sense of entitlement surrounding the franchise is so profound that the 76 years in which the Canadiens did not win the Stanley Cup seem like mistakes. The self-eulogizing might be a giant bull's-eye

Although Montreal's claim as hockey's fulcrum has waned since the NHL's headquarters were relocated to New York City in 1989, it remains a glamour franchise, arguably the league's most important. The Canadiens have been the face of the league because their players have often been the faces of the game, men who have left indelible imprints on hockey.

There are 44 Canadiens players (and 10 builders) in the Hockey Hall of Fame. Included in the initial Hall of Fame class, in 1945, was Howie Morenz, the Stratford Streak, a dashing skater and stickhandler who took his place in the pantheon of the 1920s Golden Age of Sport along with Babe Ruth, Jack Dempsey, Red Grange, Bill Tilden and Bobby Jones. Morenz's career overlapped with the end of Phantom Joe Malone's, the forward who melded production—he would be the second-leading goal scorer in pro hockey's first half century—with clean play, a combination that would be echoed decades later by the most respected man in Canada, Jean Béliveau. The Canadiens have never actually cornered the market on class; it just sometimes seemed that way.

Montreal has also had tempestuous stars, of course. If Gordie Howe is Mr. Hockey, his contemporary and rival right wing, Maurice Richard, was Mr. Quebec. In addition to being the best player, blue line in, in NHL history, the Rocket was a galvanizing figure, a man who, by dint of circumstances, became the standard-bearer for a province, a personification of its hopes and its grievances. The combustible mix erupted on March 17, 1955,

hockey's ever-shifting landscape. Well before Bobby Orr, defenseman Doug Harvey was rushing the puck. (Last year I asked Tom Johnson, a Norris Trophy–winning defenseman with Montreal from 1947 through '63 who would later coach Orr in Boston, if Harvey was second only to Orr among blueliners he had seen. Johnson—who has since passed away—replied, "I wouldn't say that." He meant that Harvey was Orr's equal.) When Jacques Plante donned a mask in a game on Nov. 1, 1959, he paved the way for his goaltending progeny to protect themselves—and truly changed the faces of hockey. Plante didn't invent the mask, just as Roy didn't invent the butterfly technique when he broke into the league in the mid 1980s. Yet it was Roy, the prickly backstop of Montreal's last two Cups, in

Roy (right), who popularized the butterfly technique, had a big impact on the league, as did (from left) Harvey, a pioneering defenseman, Gentleman Jean Béliveau and the viscerally appealing Lafleur.

in the infamous Richard Riot, one of the red-letter dates in franchise history. (The trigger: NHL president Clarence Campbell suspended Richard for the rest of the season for allegedly intentionally trying to injure Boston's Hal Laycoe and for knocking a linesman unconscious with a punch, both during a March 13 game, effectively depriving the Rocket of a chance at the scoring title.) Another right wing, Guy Lafleur, would follow a decade later, stirring Montreal passions in less inflammatory ways. Like the Rocket, the Flower was the most viscerally appealing player of his day, a skater who attracted eyeballs with his speed and flowing blond hair the way he did praise.

If the Canadiens became the cornerstone of the NHL, many who wore the uniform were prime movers in

1986 and '93, who popularized the predominant style of goaltending worldwide.

To grasp the significance of Canadiens players, consider that since the 1967 NHL expansion, they have won 33 individual awards. The other heritage franchise in Canada, the Toronto Maple Leafs, has three—and not a Hart or Norris trophy among them. (You can't write about the Canadiens without at least one snide reference to the Maple Leafs.)

So sit back and enjoy the continuing Hab-a-thon, a season in which the NHL alphabet starts with the letters *C* and *H*. And if 2008–09 at times seems a little Canadiens-centric and the nonstop fete a little too precious, realize that in the sporting firmament, this unique franchise is a shining star.   □

CIRCA 1930 | **HOWIE MORENZ JERSEY**
His number 7 was the first Habs
jersey to be retired, in 1937.

1937 | **TOE BLAKE JERSEY**
Blake's crew fell 6–5 in a
benefit for the late Hab.

1938 | **CECIL HART CARDIGAN**
Montreal was 18-17-13,
but its coach had style.

THE TRE

The fashions have changed, the sticks have curved and the goalie gear—constant over 100 years of Canadiens hockey: They keep on winning.

Photographs by DAVE SANDFORD/HOCKEY HALL OF FAME

1946 | **TOE BLAKE 200TH GOAL STICK**
Before becoming a coach, Blake scored 235 goals, his 200th with this stick.

1971 | **JEAN BÉLIVEAU FINAL-GOAL STICK**
Béliveau bid the NHL adieu by netting one in a Game 4 finals win.

1975 | **GUY LAFLEUR STICK**
This Koho kicked off a string of six straight 50-goal, 100-point seasons.

2004 | **JOSÉ THÉODORE ALL-STAR GAME GOALIE STICK**
Montreal's Sher-handed keeper stopped 10 of 12 in the win for the East.

1960s | **GUMP WORSLEY GOALIE STICK**
The decade saw four Stanley Cups and two Vézina trophies for the Gumper.

1925 | **GEORGES VÉZINA FINAL-GAME GOALIE STICK**
Vézina was wielding this lumber when he collapsed due to fatal tuberculosis.

1979 | BOB GAINEY JERSEY

Gainey battled the Soviets in the '79 Challenge Cup.

1989 | LARRY ROBINSON JERSEY

Worn in his last game as a Hab, a finals loss to Calgary.

2006 | SAKU KOIVU JERSEY

The captain's uniform from the '06 Hall of Fame Game.

ASURES

well, thank goodness that's evolved. However, one thing has remained
And we've got the hardware to prove it | COMPILED BY ADAM DUERSON

1957
JACQUES PLANTE VÉZINA TROPHY
This award was Plante's second of five straight, an unprecedented feat.

1930
MARTY BURKE TROPHY
Presented to the Canadiens defenseman by Club St. Denis following a finals win over the Bruins.

1923
ORIGINAL HART TROPHY
Donated by David Hart (the father of Canadiens coach Cecil Hart), this version was used until 1960.

1934
AURÈLE JOLIAT TROPHY
British Consols named Joliat the team's Most Useful Player in '34, when he scored 22 goals.

BRITISH CONSOLS
CIGARETTES TROPHY
WON BY
AURELE JOLIAT
1933-1934

PRESENTED TO THE PLAYER JUDGED THE MOST USEFUL TO
THE CANADIEN HOCKEY CLUB

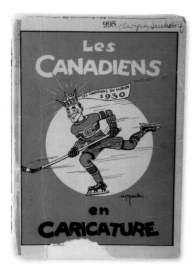

1930–31

Morenz's Habs would be *Les Champions du Monde* again, the second NHL titlists to repeat.

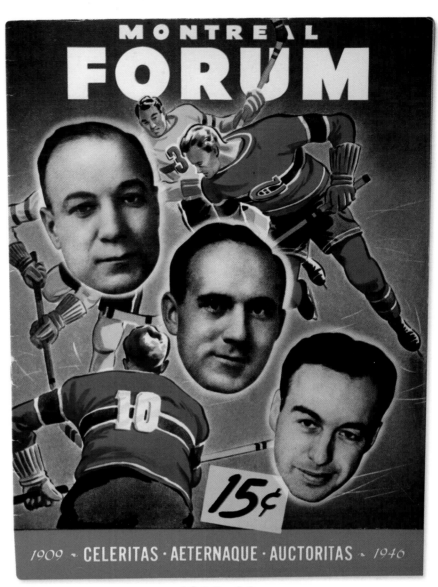

1945–46

The Cup-winning '46 squad was a sight to behold, from first-team All-Stars Bill Durnan, Maurice Richard and Émile Bouchard to Lady Byng winner Blake and coach Dick Irvin.

1933–34

The crosstown rival Maroons won 1–0 but didn't survive the decade. They folded in '38.

1937–38

A Forum crowd paid respects to Morenz on Nov. 2, 1937, eight months after his death.

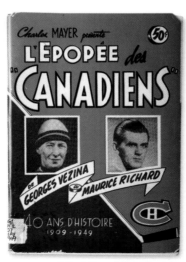

1948–49

The Epic of the Canadiens recalled 40 years, six Cups and countless future Hall of Famers.

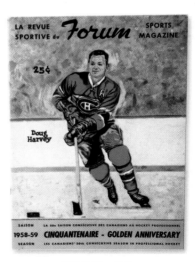

1958–59

The club toasted a golden anniversary, then raised silver (the Stanley Cup) at year's end.

1957
MAURICE RICHARD
500TH GOAL PUCK

Richard, 36, was the
NHL's oldest player
when he sank this one.

1940s
DURNAN BELLY PAD

This leather get-up makes it easy
to imagine why seven seasons
was plenty for Durnan, who won
six Vézina trophies in that time.

1959
PLANTE FIRST GOALIE MASK
Blake fumed when Plante donned this, the first mask worn in an NHL game. But a subsequent 18-game winning streak made Blake a believer.

1925
VÉZINA GOALIE SKATES
Vézina was wearing these metal-and-leather skates on that same tragic day in '25. He would die the following March, at age 39.

CIRCA 1930
JOLIAT CAP
The Little Giant kept his balding dome warm— and hidden—beneath this signature cap.

1969–70
WORSLEY PADS
Following a fourth Cup in Montreal, Worsley took these pads to Minnesota, where he played four more years.

The 1912–13 Club Athlétique Canadien were bold in stripes, although goalie Georges Vézina looked wary of the dog on Jack Laviolette's lap.

THE PRE

WAR YEARS

HALLOWED GROUND

BY E.M. SWIFT

TELL YOU A TRUE STORY. FELLA WAS AROUND here last week asking questions of one of the ushers. What is it about the Montreal Forum? the gent inquired. What makes it so special, eh? The 1992–93 season, the visitor noted, marks the 32nd time in the Forum's 69-year history that the place has hosted the Stanley Cup finals.

So, he wanted to know, what's the secret?

The usher—red coat, white shirt, black tie, black trousers: best-dressed ushers in hockey—gave it to the man straight. "It's the ghosts," he said with a smile.

I got a kick out of that. Surely did.

Maybe you've heard of me. Howie Morenz, the Stratford Streak, at your service. Keeper of the flame at the temple of hockey, heavenly rabble-rouser, unofficial recorder of Forum facts and minutiae, angel-in-waiting. I guess that over the last 69 years I've pretty much seen it all in the most storied and gloried building in hockey.

I helped open her the night of Nov. 29, 1924: Montreal Canadiens versus Toronto St. Patricks. Couple of funny things about that. The Forum wasn't our home ice. It was the spanking-new home of an NHL expansion franchise named the Montreal Maroons, who were opening on the road in Boston. We, the Canadiens, usually played at the Mount Royal Arena. But that year the arena was in the process of installing artificial-ice-making machinery, and our ice wasn't yet fit for play.

We were the defending champions, so the owners of the Forum invited us to play our home opener in their $1.5 million, 9,300-seat facility, the biggest arena in the city. "Palatial quarters," the Montreal *Gazette* called it.

The Forum was a beauty, all right: peaked stone facade, huge glass windows beneath a row of elegant arches along Atwater Avenue, a handsome marquee.

We drew 9,000 that opening game, just shy of a sellout, the largest crowd to see a hockey game in Montreal to that date. Many were still filing in when, 55 seconds into the game, my old linemate, Billy Boucher, scored the first goal in the Forum's history. Boucher had a hat trick, and we went on to an easy 7–1 win over the St. Pats. Humbly I report that I tallied once that opening night in the Forum.

The Club de Hockey Canadien moved into the Forum permanently in 1926, a year in which the archrival Maroons won the first of their two Stanley Cups.

What a rivalry it was! The Maroons were the choice of Montreal's English-speaking community, the Canadiens the team of the French. What was I, of German-Swiss descent from western Ontario, doing on a team of flying Frenchmen? Loving it. We were united by the language of hockey. Three times I was named the league's

The ice castle on the corner of Atwater and St. Catherine (left, in 1924, and above, in 1950) would grow from a capacity of 9,300 to almost 18,000. | *Photograph by* IHA/ICON SMI

MVP, and three times I helped hoist the Stanley Cup. But then . . . on Jan. 28, 1937, I caught the blade of my skate in the crevice between the ice and the boards during a game against Chicago. With Earl Seibert checking me, I fell and twisted my leg, breaking it in two places.

I never got out of the hospital. Lord knows I tried. Tried too hard, I guess. I had a nervous breakdown after being in there for a month. Deep down I must have known my career was over. On March 8, five weeks after my last game, I was sitting up in my bed, having a conversation with a friend, when I crumpled over and died of a heart attack. Some said of a broken heart. Who knows?

Shocked. That was the reaction in Montreal. Three days after my death the team held a memorial service for me at the Forum, during which they placed my body at center ice. The Canadiens, Maroons and Maple Leafs were all seated around me, and a floral number 7 adorned my casket.

Fifteen thousand fans sat in silence. It was an eerie scene, believe me. Another 10,000 gathered outside on St. Catherine Street, and thousands more lined the route to the Mount Royal Cemetery, where they laid my body to rest. The service was broadcast over the radio, and the chaplain called me "the greatest of them all." I heard every word. I was up there in the Forum rafters, feeling sorry for myself and wishing like hell I'd cut in on Seibert instead of trying to beat him along the boards.

"Hello, Howie."

It was Georges Vézina, welcoming me to the rafters. He had been our goaltender for nine years. He led the league in '24–25 with a 1.87 goals-against average. What reflexes he had! But in the first game of the '25–26 season he collapsed with a high fever after the first period; he was spitting blood. They took him to the hospital, and four months later, on March 27, 1926, he died of tuberculosis.

"Hello, Georges," I said. "This isn't. . . ."

"Heaven? No, Howie. It's the Forum."

I reached over to touch him, and my hand went right through his. "Still a sieve," I teased. "So, what's next?"

"We're to be here for a while," said Georges. "Kind of watch over the boys. It's fun."

Vézina was right. The years flew by so fast, we couldn't keep track of them. How many times did I sit up there among the banners and cheer the Punch Line of Toe Blake, Rocket Richard and Elmer Lach—the most famous scoring unit in Canadiens history? I remember Richard's 50 goals in 50 games in '44–45 as if it were yesterday. Young Jean Béliveau. Crafty Doug Harvey. Boom Boom Geoffrion, who married Marlene, my only daughter.

When the original Forum was just a skating rink, fans could pay 35 cents to see the Canadiens' first-ever game, at the Jubilee Arena on Jan. 5, 1910. The 1924–25 team (right) had five future Hall of Famers, including Vézina (left), as well as Boucher (far left), who scored the first goal at the Forum.

Management kept fancying up the place. First thing Mr. Frank Selke did when he became general manager of the Canadiens in 1946 was get rid of the Millionaires' section at the north end of the arena. Bleacher seats, that's what the Millionaires' section really was, 50 cents a seat. A chain-link fence kept the bleacherites from mingling with the tonier gents in the good seats.

By 1949, the Forum's silver anniversary, management had added the blue section, increasing the grand old dame's seating capacity to 13,551. Richard was in his prime then, and the tempestuous Rocket owned the city as no Canadiens player has before or since. He shattered the league scoring record, finishing his career with 544 goals. We won five straight Stanley Cups, from 1956 through '60, with Richard—a record string that still stands.

In 1968, at a cost of $10 million, the Forum was completely renovated to the form it retains today. The demolition crews moved in hours after we had swept the St. Louis Blues for coach Toe Blake's eighth Stanley Cup, another NHL record. Everything was replaced but the seats. New roof, lobby, concourses, escalators, plus that awful new boxlike exterior. Inside, though, the old girl looked better than ever. The 16,197 seats seemed to hang right over the ice.

Another 1,700 standing-room tickets were made available for each game. It's quite a show when the ushers open the doors for the standing-room patrons. Young, old, men, women sprint for their favorite spot as if there were a pot of dreams waiting for them inside.

Perhaps there is. There's hardly a citizen in Montreal who can't tell you when he went inside the Forum for the first time. "There's only going to be one Forum," says the great Guy Lafleur. "This place is like church for a lot of fans across Canada."

Sometimes people think they see us. Ghosts in Canadiens sweaters. Montreal players sometimes think they see us in the dressing room. Our faces are all up on the wall—37 Canadiens [now 44] who've been elected to the Hall of Fame. The names of every other player on every Canadiens roster since our first NHL season, in 1917–18, are on plaques on those walls. And above our pictures is that marvelous line from *In Flanders Fields*, written in '15 by John McCrae, a Canadian poet who was also a surgeon at a Montreal hospital: *To you from failing hands we throw the torch; be yours to hold it high.*

The boys seem to take those words pretty seriously. Year after year they've put on a pretty good show. ☐

From SPORTS ILLUSTRATED, *June 7, 1993*

In life as well as death, the three-time MVP Morenz (left) was the spirit of the Forum's early years. Following what would be a fatal leg injury, he was mourned by fans in a service at the Forum (right) and by teammates who played a memorial game in his honor and turned his locker into a shrine.

THE DAWN OF AN ICE AGE

The era of Georges Vézina, Howie Morenz and four Stanley Cups

George Hainsworth (stopping the Rangers in 1931) succeeded Vézina in goal and went on to set an NHL season record with 22 shutouts.

Founded to be a French rival of Montreal's English clubs, the Canadiens' first team featured future Hall of Famers Jack Laviolette, Newsy Lalonde and hard-shooting Didier Pitre (right).

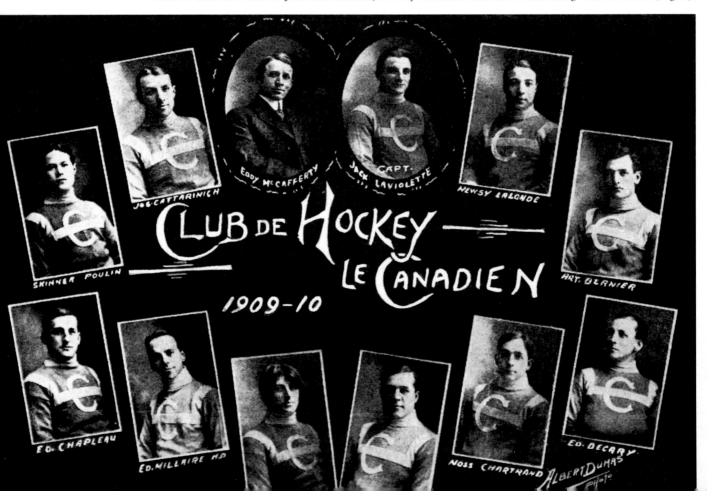

CLUB DE HOCKEY LE CANADIEN 1909-10

THE ALL-ERA TEAM

JOHN GAGNON

RIGHT WING, 1930-40 | The Black Cat was small (5' 5") but played huge for Montreal over 10 seasons, especially in the '31 Stanley Cup finals, when he scored the Cup-winning goal against Chicago. Gagnon lit the lamp 115 times and assisted on 137 goals in 406 games with the Canadiens.

HOWIE MORENZ

CENTER, 1923-34, '36-37 | The three-time Hart Trophy winner was the greatest playmaker of his time. He once held the NHL's goal-scoring record and was the game's most popular player. His appearances south of the border were instrumental in the league's growth in the United States, earning him the title of the Babe Ruth of Hockey. Morenz died on March 8, 1937, following complications from breaking a leg in a game on Jan. 28.

AURÈLE JOLIAT

LEFT WING, 1922-38 | The greatest left wing of his era and one of the league's toughest players of all time, Joliat scored 270 goals and 460 points in 644 games for the Canadiens, winning the Hart Trophy in 1934. Joliat would win three Stanley Cups with Le Bleu-Blanc-Rouge, skating alongside Morenz while wearing his trademark black cap.

SYLVIO MANTHA

DEFENSEMAN, 1923-36 | Mantha started as a forward, an experience that was critical to his becoming one of the best two-way defensemen of the NHL's first half-century. Durable (538 games in 13 Montreal seasons) and skilled (141 points), Mantha was at the heart of three Stanley Cup champs, sharing the glory in '30–31 with his younger brother, Georges.

ALBERT LEDUC

DEFENSEMAN, 1925-33, '34-35 | Speedy, strong and tough, Leduc was known as the Battleship in nine seasons with Montreal, scoring 56 goals. He then became a minor league player-coach, counting a young Hector (Toe) Blake among his charges.

GEORGES VÉZINA

GOALTENDER, 1910-25 | The netminder for Les Habs' first two Stanley Cup teams, the Chicoutimi Cucumber was hockey's iron man, playing in 328 straight regular-season games (and 39 more in the playoffs) over 16 seasons in the National Hockey Association and the early years of the NHL.

The 1934–35 team (left) had Joliat (third from right), who won the Hart Trophy in '33–34.

Les Habs won their inaugural Stanley Cup in 1915–16 (above), the 14th pro season in Montreal for defenseman Laviolette (right), who had been the first captain, coach and general manager of the Canadiens.

Montreal native Sprague Cleghorn (left) was the muscle on the 1923–24 Cup winners. Mantha (below, left) was the top defenseman on back-to-back champions ('29–30 and '30–31).

THE POST

Jacques Plante had a great view
and a view of greatness in 1957,
as the Canadiens faced off
against Boston on their way to
the second of five straight titles.

WAR 100 YEARS

THE ROCKET'S FLAIR

BY HERBERT WARREN WIND

HOCKEY IS DEEP IN THE MONTREALER'S blood. After a fine play by a member of the home team or, for that matter, of the visiting team, the Forum reverberates from the rinkside to the rafters with enthusiastic applause. But many volts above this in feeling and many decibels above in volume is the singular and sudden pandemonium that shatters the Forum, like thunder and lightning, whenever the incomparable star of Les Canadiens, Maurice (the Rocket) Richard, fights his way through the enemy defense and blasts the puck past the goalie. There is no sound quite like it in the whole world of sport.

A powerfully built athlete of 33 who stands 5' 10" and now weighs 180, having put on about a pound a year since breaking in with Les Canadiens in 1942, Joseph Henri Maurice Richard, handsome and intense, is generally regarded by most aficionados, be they Montrealers or *étrangers*, as the greatest player in the history of hockey.

Whether he is or not, of course, is one of those sports arguments that boil down to a matter of personal opinion. As Richard's supporters invariably point out, however, hockey is in essence a game of scoring, and here there can be no argument: The Rocket stands in a class by himself. Flip through the pages of the record book. Most Goals: 384, set by Maurice Richard in 12 seasons (with the next man, Nels Stewart, a full 60 goals away); Most Goals in One Season: 50, set by Maurice Richard in a 50-game schedule in '44–45; Most Goals in a Playoff Series: 12, Maurice Richard; Most Goals in a Playoff Game: 5, Maurice Richard; Longest Consecutive Scoring Streak: at least one goal in nine consecutive games, Maurice Richard; and so on and on. The record book supplies no entry for Most Winning Goals, but several Montreal fans who lovingly compile all Richardiana can document that by the beginning of the season, their man had scored the goal that won no fewer than 59 regular-season games and eight playoff games.

It is not simply the multiplicity of Richard's goals or their timeliness but, rather, the spectacular manner in which he scores them that has made the fiery rightwinger the Babe Ruth of Hockey. "There are goals, and there are Richard goals," Dick Irvin, the old Silver Fox who has coached the Canadiens for the length of Richard's career, remarked. "He doesn't get lucky goals. He can get to a puck and do things to it quicker than any man I've ever seen—even if he has to lug two defensemen with him, and he frequently has to. And his shots! They go in with such velocity."

FRANK PRAZAK/HOCKEY HALL OF FAME

Richard (opposite and top, left, with Punch Linemates Blake and Lach) carved a spot in hockey history with his 50 goals in 50 games. | *Photograph by* DAVID BIER

ONE OF THE POPULAR INDOOR PASTIMES YEAR-ROUND in Montreal is talking over old Richard goals—which one you thought was the most neatly set up, which one stirred you the most, etc.—much in the way Americans used to hot-stove about Ruth's home runs and do today about Willie Mays's various catches. In Irvin's opinion—and Hector (Toe) Blake and Elmer Lach, Richard's teammates on the famous Punch Line also feel this way—the Rocket's most sensational goal was the Seibert goal, in the 1945–46 season. Earl Seibert, a 225-pound defenseman who was playing for Detroit that season, hurled himself at Richard as he swept on a solo into the Detroit zone. Richard occasionally will bend his head and neck very low when he is trying to outmaneuver a defenseman. He did on this play. The two collided with a thud, and as they straightened up, there was Richard, still on his feet, still controlling the puck and, sitting on top of his shoulders, the burly Seibert. Richard not only carried Seibert with him on the way to the net, but with tremendous extra effort, faked the goalie out of position and with his free hand managed to hoist the puck into the far corner of the cage.

There are two interesting epilogues to this story. The first concerns Seibert and serves well to illustrate the enormous respect in which Richard is held by opposing players. When Seibert clambered into the dressing room after the game, Jack Adams, the voluble Detroit coach, eyed him scornfully. "Why, you dumb Dutchman," he began, "you go let that Richard. . . ." "Listen, Mr. Adams," Seibert cut in, "any guy who can carry me 60 feet and then put the puck into the net—well, more power to him!" And that ended that. The second rider to the story is that Richard is certainly the only hockey player who, to increase his ability to operate with a burden, has frequently spent an extra half hour after the regular practice sessions careering full steam around the rink with his young son, Maurice Jr., the Petit Rocket, perched on his shoulders.

There is no question that Richard's most heroic winning goal was the Boston goal—the one he scored against the Bruins in 1952 to lift Montreal into the finals of the Stanley Cup playoffs. It came late in the third period of a 1–1 game. Early in that period Maurice received a deep gash over his left eye. He was taken to the clinic inside the Forum, and the cut was hastily patched up. Blood was still trickling down from the dressing when he returned to the bench and took his next turn on the ice. "I can see that goal now," Frank Selke Jr., the son of the Canadiens' managing director, reminisced recently. "Richard sets off a chain reaction whenever he gets the puck, even if it is just a routine pass. It's strange

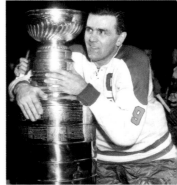

Toting a defenseman (left), or out on his own (below, beating the Bruins' Red Henry in 1953), the Rocket powered his way to the net and carried Montreal to eight Stanley Cups—while sharing the ride with the Petit Rocket, teammates and (far right, after his 500th goal, in '57) the fans.

and wonderful, the way he communicates with the crowd. Now, this time he got the puck at our own blue line, and you knew—everybody knew—that the game was over right then. Here's what he did. He slipped around Woody Dumart, who was the check, and set sail down the righthand boards. Bill Quackenbush and Bob Armstrong, the Boston defensemen, were ready for him. He swung around Armstrong with a burst of speed, using his right hand to carry the puck and fending off Armstrong with his left, but Quackenbush pinned him into the boards in the corner. And then, somehow, he broke away from Quackenbush, skated across in front of the net, pulled Jim Henry out of the goal, and drove it home."

AS BEFITS THE BABE RUTH OF HOCKEY, RICHARD IS the highest-paid player in the history of the game. While Les Canadiens' front office prefers not to divulge his exact salary, it amounts to a very healthy chunk of his estimated annual income of $50,000, which is filled out by his commissions for endorsing such products as a hair tonic and the Maurice Richard–model wind jacket, his cut from the sale of *Le Rocket du Hockey* and other publications about him, and his occasional appearances during the off-season as a wrestling referee. A few years ago Richard and his teammate

Kenny Reardon dropped in for lunch at the Canadian Club, a restaurant in Montreal. "When the other diners spotted Rocket," Reardon relates, "they began to pass the hat for him. It was a spontaneous gesture of appreciation. They collected $50, just like that. People can't do enough for him." Richard, in consequence, is the perfect companion to travel with anywhere in Quebec. No one will let him pay for a meal, for lodgings, for transportation, for anything.

And what about Le Rocket? How does he react to this fantastic adulation? Perhaps the surest key is the way he conducts himself after he scores one of his roof-raising goals. Down on the ice, below the tumult of tribute, Richard, while the referee is waiting for the clamor to subside before dropping the puck for the next face-off, cruises solemnly in slow circles, somewhat embarrassed by the strength of the ovation, his normally expressive dark eyes fixed expressionless on the ice. In his actions there is never the suspicion of the idol recognizing the plaudits of his fans. The slow circles that Richard describes after he has scored serve a distinct purpose for him. They add up to a brief moment of uncoiling, one of the few he is able to allow himself during the six-month-long season. "Maurice," Toe Blake once remarked, "lives to score goals." □

From SPORTS ILLUSTRATED, *December 6, 1954*

GALLERY

GREATEST GENERATION

After 12 dry seasons a new breed of Canadiens drank from the Cup seven times

Along with the Rocket, Hector (Toe) Blake (far left, collecting the 1946 Lady Byng Trophy) and center Elmer Lach (near left) gave the Punch Line its pop.

Saving face: After his face was cut in a 1959 game against the Rangers, Plante got patched up and went right back in, becoming the first NHL goalie to wear a mask in a game.

Bill Durnan played just seven years in the NHL, but the ambidextrous goalie won six Vézina Trophies and in 1949 set an NHL record with four consecutive shutouts.

Dick Irvin took over the Canadiens in 1940 and built the once proud franchise back into a winner. During his 15 seasons behind the bench he led Montreal to three Stanley Cup titles.

With his thundering slap shot, Bernie (Boom Boom) Geoffrion was a key link for the Habs for 14 seasons.

Burly but slick-skating Johnson, the 1959 Norris Trophy winner, was on six Stanley Cup champion Montreal teams.

The Habs of the '50s were a formidable bunch. Here, in '57, Toronto faced (from left) Claude Provost, Don Marshall, Harvey, Dollard St. Laurent and Plante.

CLOCKWISE FROM RIGHT: IMPERIAL OIL-TUROFSKY/HOCKEY HALL OF FAME (2); YALE JOEL/TIME LIFE PICTURES/GETTY IMAGES; IMPERIAL OIL-TUROFSKY/HOCKEY HALL OF FAME

Four days after suspending Richard for the rest of the season and the playoffs following a fight on March 13, 1955, NHL president Clarence Campbell was greeted at the Forum by angry fans. The ensuing "Richard Riot" remains a watershed moment in Canadiens, and Canadian, history.

Plante (in net) and Harvey (2) got down to business in the 1959 Stanley Cup finals, stopping this Maple Leafs shot to help Montreal clinch its fourth straight Cup with a 5–3 Game 5 win.

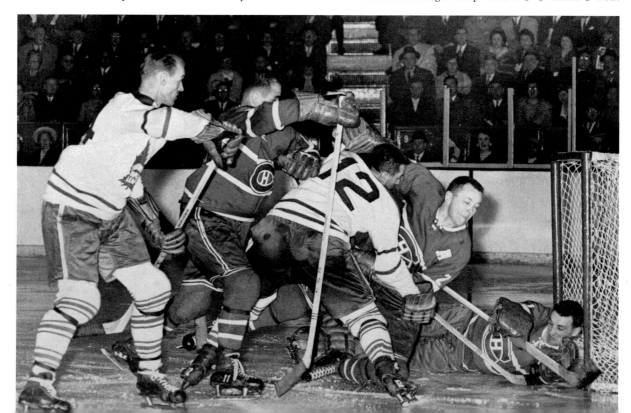

THE ALL-ERA TEAM

MAURICE RICHARD

RIGHT WING, 1942-60 | Famed for his skill and feistiness, the marquee player of his era became the first to score 50 goals in 50 games in 1944–45, one of five times he'd top the NHL in goals. The Rocket was the first player to reach 500 goals in a career and held the career goals record from 1952 until Gordie Howe broke it in 1963.

JEAN BÉLIVEAU

CENTER, 1950-51, '52-71 | Nobody's name is engraved more times on the Stanley Cup than Béliveau's, who was part of 10 championship teams as a player and seven more as an executive with the Canadiens. A two-time Hart Trophy winner and the inaugural Conn Smythe Trophy winner, in '71, Béliveau retired as the NHL's alltime postseason scoring leader.

DICKIE MOORE

LEFT WING, 1951-63 | Digging Dickie was always working on the ice, and it showed in the results. Moore led the league in goals and points in 1957–58 despite playing with a broken wrist for three months. A year later he set a league record with 96 points. The Hall of Famer was part of six Cup title teams and played in the All-Star Game three times.

DOUG HARVEY

DEFENSEMAN, 1947-61 | A dominant defenseman both with and without the puck, Harvey's skating and stickhandling made him an integral part of the Canadiens' dynasty of the 1950s. He won the Norris Trophy in six of his final seven seasons with Montreal, a streak interrupted only by teammate Tom Johnson in 1958–59.

TOM JOHNSON

DEFENSEMAN, 1947-48, '49-63 | Only three defensemen played in more games for Montreal than the 1970 Hall of Fame inductee. Overshadowed for most of his career by Harvey, the spectacular two-way defenseman and two-time All-Star remains 11th in points and 12th in assists alltime among Canadiens defenders.

JACQUES PLANTE

GOALTENDER, 1952-63 | During his Canadiens tenure Jake the Snake developed and introduced the goaltending mask and was the first to regularly skate behind the net to play the puck. He holds the Montreal records for games (556) and wins (312) and ranks second in shutouts (58) and goals-against average (2.23).

The Rocket's younger brother Henri, another Canadiens hero, twice led the league in assists.

Toe Blake, now a coach, got a hoist from Moore (left) and Geoffrion after Montreal won another Cup in '56.

Harvey (below with puck and above on knees) reigned as the NHL's top defenseman in 14 years as a Hab.

In what was a familiar sight in the '60s, the Canadiens celebrated in the Forum after winning the 1965 Stanley Cup.

THE 1960s

MEET GENTLEMAN JEAN

BY WHITNEY TOWER

LAST SUMMER, SHORTLY AFTER HE HAD LEFT HIS 15-year job as coach of the Montreal Canadiens to accept a similar position with the Chicago Blackhawks, Dick Irvin was asked which of the six teams in the NHL was most likely to win the 1955–56 league championship. "That's easy," replied Irvin. "Montreal, by 10 games." ❡ A few days ago Irvin's successor, Hector (Toe) Blake, reflected on the curious position in which Irvin's departure had left him. "If we finish anywhere but first, I'll feel I've done a very bad job," Blake said. "If things go right, yes, we should win by 10 games. But any hockey man will tell you that in hockey, things don't always go right."

Despite this typical Blake-like pessimism, he stands today in what must be one of the most enviable positions ever held by a professional coach in any sport. Blake can boast something no other team has: the two best scorers in hockey. One is Maurice (Rocket) Richard. The other is a strikingly handsome young man who answers to the name of Jean Béliveau. It is quite possible that no hockey team in history has ever been led by two such brilliant craftsmen. It is likewise probable that no two stars on the same team were ever so exactly opposite in temperament as are Richard and Béliveau.

As the onetime leftwinger on the famous Montreal Punch Line, with Elmer Lach at center and Richard at his customary right wing position, Blake probably knows the Rocket as well as any man ever will. When he talks of his friend and star today, it is with a deep and far-reaching feeling of fondness and unashamed admiration. "As long as I live, I know I'll never see a player like Maurice. He lives for only one thing: to put that puck in the net."

As for Béliveau, this is Blake's first season of close association with the 24-year-old center, who is leading the league in scoring, and he is understandably less inclined to employ full use of superlatives. "I think Jean is great," he says. "He is big and strong and can do everything well, but he doesn't have the desire to score that Maurice has." Tommy Ivan, general manager for Chicago, gives a more thorough appraisal of Béliveau's talents. "Béliveau is great because he takes the direct route. No long way around for him. He has the size [6' 3"] and the weight [205 pounds] to hold his own. He's tremendously strong, a beautiful skater, already a superb stickhandler, strictly a team man with a perfect sense of playmaking. He has

In 1965 Béliveau led Montreal to the Stanley Cup championship (left) and won the inaugural Conn Smythe Trophy as playoff MVP. | *Photograph by* JOSEPH CONSENTINO

JAMES DRAKE

a wonderfully hard and accurate shot. He'd be a star on any hockey club. I wish he were on mine."

The reasons for Béliveau's presence today on the Canadiens' first line are basically the same that can be found to explain the emergence of Montreal in the past few years as the dominant force in Canadian hockey. Like thousands of youngsters before and after him, young Jean, as a boy in Victoriaville, Que., and later in the city of Quebec, indulged in the hero worship of Rocket Richard. Unlike the majority of his contemporary hero worshippers, young Jean had tremendous natural talent of his own—a talent that quickly became recognized across the Dominion when he graduated from the juniors to stardom as a $20,000-a-year "amateur" center with the Quebec Aces.

When officials of Les Canadiens were trying to persuade him—after a dazzling five goals during a three-game tryout on the big team during the 1952–53 season—that he could earn more than $20,000 by signing a Montreal contract, it remained for his idol, the Rocket, to clinch the deal. Béliveau recalled the incident not long ago in his heavy French accent. "Maurice say to me, 'Jean, you come with us and we have a good time. You like playing for Les Canadiens.' Today I am happy I do what he say."

The Rocket is apparently happy too, for now, after having Béliveau as a teammate for three seasons, he is more of an admirer than ever. The other night he paid the young star what must rank as one of hockey's highest compliments: "He gets along with everyone, and he's the best center I've seen since I've been in the league." And Frank J. Selke, the club's managing director, says of Béliveau, "He is so modest that he blushes when anybody says anything nice about him."

Béliveau's modesty makes it easy for him to minimize his own accomplishments. "If people are saying I am good, it is nice to hear. But to play good hockey, you must be lucky to be born with ability. Then you work hard at it the rest of the time. I work hard for my job, and I think this team is good one. We are big happy family here."

Béliveau should be a member of the big happy family for the next 10 years. As a drawing power second only to Richard, Béliveau could earn more than $25,000 this season, not including the $10,000 he is reportedly pulling in for his role as a sort of roving goodwill ambassador for a Montreal brewery. He and his pretty wife, Elsie, have recently moved into a new house, and one of their present off-duty preoccupations is the selection of a suite of furniture—a three-year-overdue gift from the club management, which took this method of showing him its

Béliveau was a fan favorite not only for his playmaking ability but also for his cool demeanor on the ice. From 1950 through '71 with Montreal he scored 507 goals and a then-record 176 points in the playoffs and won 10 Stanley Cup titles.

appreciation for consenting to a Montreal tryout while he was still playing for Quebec. Less distinguished prospects on trial receive a flat payment of $100 a game.

When Les Canadiens in their red uniforms with royal blue and white trim skate out on the Forum ice to the applause from the most knowledgeable and enthusiastic audience in all sport, the autograph hunters seek out Richard first and then Béliveau. Quite in keeping with their different personalities, Richard, during this brief lull before the battle, retains his usual serious scowl. Béliveau gives his admirers a faint smile. The game under way, they remain individually different although working for the same cause.

"With Maurice," said Selke, "his moves are powered by instinctive reflexes. Maurice can't learn from lectures. He does everything by instinct and with sheer power. Béliveau, on the other hand, is probably the classiest hockey player I've ever seen. He has a flair for giving you his hockey as a master showman. He is a perfect coach's hockey player because he studies and learns. He's moving and planning all the time, thinking out the play required for each situation. The difference between the two best hockey players in the game today is simply this: Béliveau is a perfectionist, Richard is an opportunist."

As these classifications clearly suggest, the mannerisms of the two men on the ice are quite different. Richard's fiery and explosive temper has gotten him more than once into a hotbed of trouble. Béliveau, for a time, was just the opposite, and, in fact, during his first year with Les Canadiens he acquired the nickname Gentleman Jean when it was discovered around the league that the rookie had a distinct aversion to mixing it up. His former coach, Irvin, noticing the change that has come over Béliveau during the last year, says of him now, "Like the other great players in the game, Jean was quick to smarten up when he saw the opposition getting the best of him. He'll never be the type to go around looking for trouble, but now he can be as tough as anybody."

This week, as Les Canadiens tried to bear down in an effort to end the two-year NHL championship reign of the Red Wings, all hands were as optimistic as they dared be. Richard, still showing the old-time lightning reflexes that many thought would have left him by now, said he felt better than ever. Béliveau, trying to hang on to his league scoring lead, was smiling gently and still maintaining an average of better than a point a game. And Blake, true to form, was giving off the same old gloom. "If our team is playing right, they're all beautiful to watch. But any hockey man will tell you that in hockey, things don't always go right." □

From SPORTS ILLUSTRATED, *January 23, 1956*

GALLERY

COUNTER CULTURE

Wresting the Cup from Toronto, the Canadiens moved the capital of hockey to Montreal

Hall of Fame left wing Dick Duff (8) clears the puck away from goalie Charlie Hodge as J.C. Tremblay (3) and Ted Harris (10) choke off Chicago in the '65 finals.

Gump Worsley was a rock in goal in the late '60s, winning four Stanley Cups and sharing two Vézina Trophies (with Hodge and Rogie Vachon).

All signs pointed to victory for Montreal in Game 7 of the '65 finals, as Les Habs beat Chicago 4–0 for the second of their five Cups of the '60s.

As Montreal skated to the '66 title, Gilles Tremblay made sure to stick with Detroit great Gordie Howe.

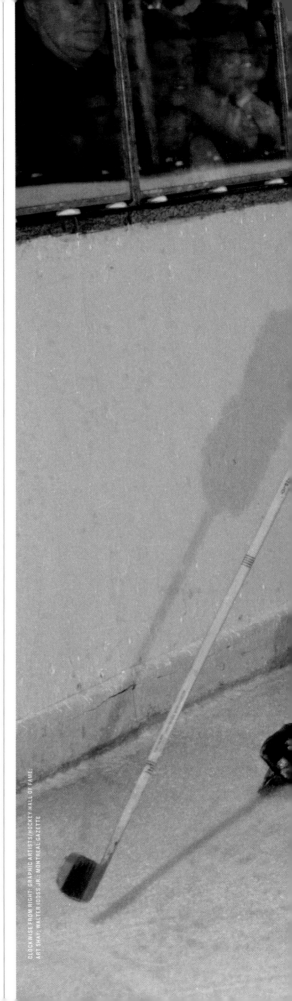

Dave Balon, Duff, Yvan Cournoyer & Co. swept
Toronto in '66 before finishing off Detroit 4–2.

J.C. Tremblay battled a Maple
Leafs player in 1967; the rival
Canadian clubs won nine Cups
between them in the 1960s.

Duff tried to score against
Detroit in '66 (below)
while Robert Rousseau
awaited the rebound.
After he scored the Cup-
winning goal in Game 6,
Henri Richard needed—
and deserved—a drink.

With Duff (8) under attack, Jean Béliveau showed his less-gentle side to the St. Louis Blues' Al Arbour in Game 1 of the '68 finals.

The '68 Cup was one of five John Ferguson would win in eight seasons in which he gave Montreal punch with his stick (303 points) and his fists (1,214 penalty minutes).

The Canadiens cleared the boards at the Game 4 buzzer to celebrate their sweep of the Blues.

THE ALL-ERA TEAM

BERNIE GEOFFRION

RIGHT WING, 1950–64 | The 11-time All-Star popularized the slap shot, earning him the famous nickname Boom Boom. In 1960–61 he joined Maurice Richard as a 50-goal scorer—the second time he led the league in goals—winning his second Art Ross Trophy and only Hart Trophy.

HENRI RICHARD

CENTER, 1955–75 | Although he was overshadowed by his brother and sometime linemate Maurice, nobody won more Stanley Cups as a player than the Pocket Rocket, who raised the silver trophy 11 times. In North American professional sports history, only Boston Celtics great Bill Russell has as many championships on his résumé as a player.

GILLES TREMBLAY

LEFT WING, 1960–69 | In his nine seasons Tremblay scored 168 goals and totaled 330 points for four championship Canadiens teams. He scored more than 20 goals in a season five times, including in 1961–62, when he had a career-high 32 while playing on a line with Geoffrion and Jean Béliveau. Forced to retire early due to asthma, Tremblay became the team's French-language color commentator.

JACQUES LAPERRIÈRE

DEFENSEMAN, 1962–74 | A rock on defense, the 6' 2" Laperrière used his unusually long reach to disrupt countless offensive rushes. In 1963–64, at the age of 22, he became just the second defenseman (and fifth Canadien overall) to capture the Calder Trophy. He added the Norris Trophy in 1966 after winning the second of his six Stanley Cups with Montreal.

J.C. TREMBLAY

DEFENSEMAN, 1959–72 | A converted left wing, Tremblay became one of the most esteemed two-way defensemen in history, being named to the All-Star team seven times while also finishing among the league's top 10 in assists twice. Although he won no major trophies, he was runner-up for the Conn Smythe in 1966 to Roger Crozier and for the Norris in '68 to Bobby Orr.

JACQUES PLANTE

GOALTENDER, 1952–63 | Plante led the league in wins and goals-against average in the championship season of 1959–60 and again in '61–62. From '59–60 through '62–63 Plante led the league in total wins (127) and winning percentage (.652).

Vachon stopped Boston in a '69 semifinal, and Montreal advanced to sweep St. Louis again.

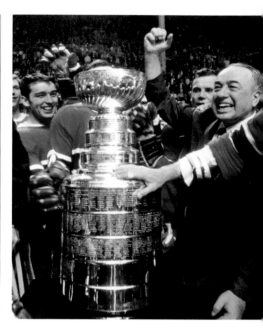

After his eighth, and final, Cup as a coach (and 11th overall), Toe Blake (right) lit up the Forum in '68.

A defensive giant in the '60s, Laperrière (here against Toronto in '69) played in five All-Star Games in 12 seasons.

Montreal's '70s show—starring Ken Dryden (in goal), Guy LaPointe (5), Réjean Houle (15) and Bob Gainey in the '78 Cup final—was an NHL hit.

DAN BALIOTTI

LAFLEUR

THE SILENT ASSASSIN

BY J.D. REED

"After all, in Montreal when one puts on that red sweater, one is a Canadien."
—JEAN BÉLIVEAU

O N THE LATE-NIGHT AIR CANADA FLIGHT to Montreal the Canadiens are celebrating a victory over the Maple Leafs with a few smuggled cartons of Molson's ale. It is a raucous time, and there is more to feel good about than just another win. The fact is, that this Montreal team has begun to approach the quality of some of its famous predecessors. Having long since clinched its divisional race, it leads the NHL with a 51-9-10 record. At week's end the Canadiens were 10 points ahead of the Philadelphia Flyers and 15 ahead of the third-place Boston Bruins, skating toward the playoffs with that old Montreal spirit. Even though there is no Richard on the team for the first time in 32 years, and even though the Forum has a few empty seats now and then and crooner Roger Doucet sings the national anthem, *O Canada*, in English as well as French, a Canadien is still a Canadien.

True, the Stanley Cup resides in Philadelphia, where Bobby Clarke & Co. would like to keep it for a third straight year. True, last season in the playoffs Montreal was knocked off its pedestal by Buffalo. Ah, but wait till this year. The Habs have a little something extra going for them.

There is Guy Lafleur, for instance. He sits amid the airborne hullabaloo over Lake Ontario holding his ale bottle as though he would like a glass in which to pour it—something more civilized, if you please, than the chug-a-lugging going on around him. In his perfectly tailored, vested blue suit, with a fashionably slender attaché case under the seat, the 24-year-old Lafleur looks like a Gallic stockbroker who has been mistakenly placed between 6' 5" Pete Mahovlich and battle-scarred team captain Yvan Cournoyer. But make no mistake about it, Lafleur is a hockey player, an extremely gifted wing. Last season he set a team record of 53 goals, and so far this season he has scored 45 goals and has 57 assists to lead the league, with Clarke in hot pursuit.

Lafleur is a reluctant superstar. Shunning the spotlight, the interview, the after-dinner speaking tours of a player of his rank, he prefers to spend most of his free time at home with his wife, Lise, and his infant son, Martin. He is a collector of watches—and indeed, he

After starting his career with three lackluster seasons, Lafleur emerged as the successor to Richard and Béliveau. | *Photograph by* DICK RAPHAEL

seems to know the value of time better than most. When he lived next door to defenseman Pierre Bouchard, he would often show up at 8 a.m., rousing his protesting teammate for an 11:30 practice. "Superfleur," as he is called in Montreal, is in the dressing room two hours before games, determinedly whacking hockey sticks against a table, and breaking several, until his nerves have calmed down and he finds sticks that won't crack. "If you aren't expecting it, that sound really makes you jump," says goalie Ken Dryden.

The son of a welder in Thurso, Que., a sleepy pulp-mill town, Lafleur set records by the handful in junior hockey, ending his stint in Quebec City with 130 goals in 62 games. Montreal's No. 1 draft choice in 1971, loudly hailed as the next Richard, the next Béliveau, Lafleur responded with three lackluster seasons. Even though he was the highest-paid youngster in the NHL at the time, his father-in-law, Roger Barry, part owner of the Quebec Nordiques, the WHA franchise, kept trying to get him to jump to that team.

"When I first saw him, I thought he was an average hockey player," says Lafleur linemate Steve Shutt. "Then two years ago in Chicago he gave us a taste of what was inside that shyness. He simply deked the entire Blackhawks team—skated through them like they weren't even on the ice. Henri Richard said, 'Did you see that? No one can do that.' After that we knew it was just a matter of getting that kind of play out of him all the time."

Lafleur's early difficulties were compounded by the fact that he could satisfy neither the sophisticated and critical Montreal fans and sportswriters nor himself. Today the French-language Montreal papers run a Lafleur story every other day, reporting every headache, every smile, and committing to history every one of his few words. But in seasons past he maintained a self-imposed silence, a reticence rarely matched outside a wax museum. "It took Guy a long time to get this thing resolved," says Béliveau, the marvelous Canadiens center of 1950–71 and a childhood idol of Lafleur's. "Now he has a 10-year contract, and he has settled down."

When Lafleur takes the ice these days, there is a sudden transformation, from shrinking violet to *mousquetaire* with cape and sword.

"Guy has all the talent in the world," says his coach, Scotty Bowman. "He skates like a genius, he's puck-hungry in the best sense, and he'll go into the corners when he has to. But he's best in front of the net.

"I think the real secret of his success is his physical condition. It's amazing. We had the team tested two years

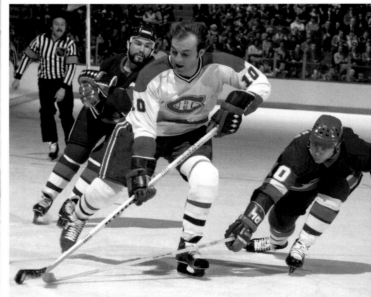

back, and Lafleur was in better shape than anyone else. He practices just as hard as he plays."

Punch Imlach, the Buffalo general manager, says, "Guy has tremendous speed. He can go from one end of the rink to the other with the best in the league, and he's amazing around the net. He is the epitome of the Montreal style."

In a recent game against the Sabres in Montreal, Lafleur's special abilities became painfully obvious to Imlach and Buffalo goaltender Gerry Desjardins. In the final 10 seconds of the second period, Cournoyer sped deep into the Sabres' zone and then was forced to throw a long back-pass. As the puck looped toward the blue line and out of play, Lafleur, astonishingly fast and agile, reached it, and while it would have been achievement enough to merely keep the puck in the zone, Lafleur managed to get off a tremendous slap shot that took the inside of the post, scoring a goal. The Forum fans exploded. "I never had a chance to move," said Desjardins later. "Anyway, it was one of those shots that I'm almost glad I didn't get a piece of. It would have hurt for a week."

So Guy Lafleur *est là*, as they say in Montreal; he's arrived, he's there. And maybe the Canadiens are, too, once again.

As the Canadiens rush toward what might turn out to be a date with Philadelphia in the Stanley Cup finals, Dryden, who didn't perform up to his best last season after returning from a year off to play legal eagle and prepare for the Canadian bar exams, is preparing his brief on the Broad Street Bullies. "Philadelphia has been able to intimidate us without intimidating us," he says. "We'd seem to be playing our game against them, but really we were not.

"This year I think Philadelphia is going to have to learn how to lose. It will be a very difficult lesson for them, and I hope it doesn't destroy their spirit."

Showing in Montreal these days is a children's adventure film called *The Mystery of the $1,000,000 Hockey Puck*, in which jewel thieves plot to smuggle diamonds into the U.S. in a Canadiens puck. Two kids overhear the plan and, in footage using real Montreal players and team broadcaster Danny Gallivan, foil the scheme. As a reward the youngsters are taken to the Canadiens' dressing room, and each is given one of those sacred red sweaters.

In such moments one can't help thinking there is more to Montreal's comeback toward hockey supremacy than Lafleur's shooting or Dryden's saves. Can the Canadiens foil the wicked Flyers of Philadelphia this spring? Only *le bon Dieu* knows for sure, and He is leaking nothing to the papers, in French or English. ☐

From SPORTS ILLUSTRATED, *March 22, 1976*

Known for his skating and presence in front of the net, Lafleur's highlights in 14 seasons with Montreal included earning the Conn Smythe Trophy after the Canadiens won the Stanley Cup in '77 (below) and, in '83, becoming just the 10th player to score 500 career goals (left).

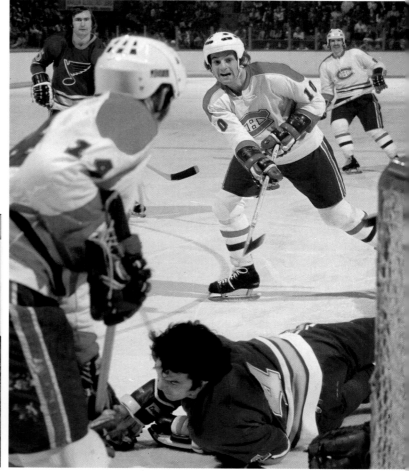

A STUDENT OF THE GAME

BY MARK MULVOY

"To be born to create, to love, to win at games is to be born to live in time of peace. But war teaches us to lose everything and become what we are not. It all becomes a question of style." —ALBERT CAMUS

KEN DRYDEN, THE McGILL UNIVERSITY LAW School student who moonlights as a goaltender for the Montreal Canadiens, contemplates the message his wife, Lynda, has hung over the desk in their apartment. "War, as I interpret it, is the variable in all men," he says. "For me, the war is hockey. I cannot let hockey make me what I am not."

Come along for a while to see how the battle goes, for Dryden is that rarest of individuals in sport, the man who does what cannot be done. Let Boston win the NHL's regular-season race in the East by 20 points. Let Chicago do the same in the West. In the heart of every Bruins and Blackhawks fan will be the secret fear that this one tall, idealistic, implacable student will rise out of the Montreal nets to rob them of the Stanley Cup, even as he did last year. It could happen. This season Kenneth Wayne Dryden has been the only bulwark between the Canadiens and certain ruin. The team

that looked so strong in October is staggering in February. But the Canadiens have lost only five of the 40 games Dryden has played. With his replacements in goal, the Canadiens have lost eight of 13 games. When Dryden came down with a back ailment at Christmas, the Canadiens were battling the Bruins and the Rangers for first place in the East. When he returned to the lineup three weeks later, they were tumbling toward fourth place. Last week it was the old, magical Dryden who braked the Canadiens' slide as he saw them through two wins and two ties on the road.

Old? He is 24 and still classed as an NHL rookie. Obviously he has not succumbed to the star syndrome, a malady that often devours the young. Except for an unlisted telephone number, Dryden's life is that of the struggling student dependent on someone else for his funds, not the pro earning a $35,000 salary.

The Drydens, who met at Cornell, live in a sparsely furnished, one-bedroom high-rise apartment in the Notre Dame de Grâce section of Montreal. The only piece of real furniture in the living room is a color television–stereo complex given Ken as Life Saver of

HEINZ KLUETMEIER

Dryden played in just 397 regular-season games but won 64.9% of them and had almost as many shutouts (46) as losses (57). | *Photograph by* STEVE BABINEAU/WIREIMAGE.COM

the Month for his Stanley Cup heroics. The dining room table is a card table in disguise, and all the chairs fold up. "You don't buy furniture impulsively," Dryden says.

When he leaves the apartment for games at the Forum or classes at McGill, Ken drives off in one of the two cars he also won for his Cup performances. Most of the Canadiens pay $35 a month to park in a covered area across the street from the Forum. Not Dryden. He cruises the streets until he spots a free parking place.

Dryden has always been a sensible human being, except maybe when he chose to become a goaltender in the first place. He started in the nets in Islington, Ont., when he was five. His father, Murray, built goals from two-by-fours and chicken wire and placed them in the driveway so the boys in the neighborhood could play ball hockey. "I played one goal, and my brother, Dave [now with the Buffalo Sabres], played the other," Ken says. "That's all there was to it."

Dryden started playing organized hockey in an Atom League when he was seven years old, with Humber Valley of Toronto's West End. The next year he played for the Humber Valley team in a Peewee League, even though he was two or three years younger than his teammates. "My father did that intentionally," Dryden says. "His feeling was that you improve more by playing against older competition. And I always managed to do all right."

Dryden played goal for Humber Valley teams until he was 15, then moved into Junior B hockey with the Etobicoke Indians. After his first season with Etobicoke he was drafted by Montreal. "I remember the night well," says Scotty Bowman, now the Montreal coach but then a scout for the team. "We knew about him from Roger Neilson, our Toronto-area scout, but we were sort of concerned about his ambition. He kept talking about going to school instead of playing Junior A."

"They wanted me to go to Peterborough, Ontario," Dryden says. "They had a strong team there but needed a second goaltender. But my schooling was the hang-up. I was planning to attend grade 13, and there would be a lot of pressure on me to do well in the classroom. I could not see how living away, playing hockey and trying to go to school in Peterborough would work, so I stayed in Toronto."

Besides playing goal for Etobicoke, Dryden was also an all-city forward on his school basketball team. In fact, when he finished grade 13, several Canadian colleges and at least one American school approached him with scholarship offers on which he could combine hockey and basketball. But Ken seemed intent on attending Princeton. Later, at the urging of friends, he visited Cornell and forgot about Princeton.

With his agile mind and body, the 6' 4" Dryden (in the McGill law library at left) continually frustrated would-be goal scorers and led the Canadiens to six Stanley Cups in seven full seasons while winning the Vézina Trophy five times.

On the ice at Cornell, Dryden was something of a legend. In three years he played in only four losing games, and his goals-against average was a microscopic 1.60.

All this time Dryden heard nothing from the Canadiens. "I never even knew they were alive," he says, "until the end of my senior year after a game at Boston College. Someone told me that [Canadiens executive] Toe Blake was in the stands." Later, Montreal G.M. Sam Pollock drove down to Ithaca, watched Dryden win another game and told him that the Canadiens would be in touch after the playoffs. Dryden had been accepted at Harvard Law School and, as he says, "I really wanted to go there." The drawback was that he could not have played hockey. Meanwhile, the Canadian national team had offered a three-year contract that included full tuition at the University of Manitoba at Winnipeg. Pollock was talking minor league hockey, nothing more.

Dryden eventually decided to play with the national team and attend law school in Winnipeg. "When I phoned Mr. Pollock," Ken says, "he was stunned. I'm sure that he thought I was using the law school approach as a lever to get more money." If anything, Dryden's seriousness about the pursuit of law impressed Pollock, and when the national team folded a year later, he offered Dryden an opportunity to combine hockey and law school in Montreal.

Ken jumped at the chance. Last season he was a full-time law student at McGill and a weekend goaltender for the Montreal Voyageurs of the American Hockey League until early in March, when the Canadiens realized they would get no Stanley Cup with the goalies then playing. Enter Dryden. Exit Boston, Minnesota and Chicago.

While Dryden has managed to combine his two careers with no apparent difficulty, he feels that the hockey world regards him with suspicion. "They have this great myth that anyone who has anything else to do obviously does not approach hockey with the proper frame of mind, but to me it's the exact opposite. Hockey as a 24-hour job, 365 days a year, is absurd."

Still, most hockey people do believe that Dryden will play two or three more years and then settle into a padded chair in a law office somewhere in Ontario. "Jeez, Murphy," Ken says, "that's such a defensive attitude, based on faulty reasoning. What they are doing is demeaning athletics. They're saying, 'Of course he won't stay around very long because he can do something else.' Certainly there are more meaningful things in life, but at the same time hockey is enjoyable and a challenge. That's why I play it. Believe me, I couldn't live with law alone." □

From SPORTS ILLUSTRATED, *February 14, 1973*

GALLERY

DECADE OF DOMINANCE

With six Stanley Cup titles, the 1970s was the most successful period in franchise history

In a rare 1975 clash against the Soviet Central Red Army team, Doug Risebrough and Montreal managed a 3–3 tie.

In 1973 Henri Richard raised a final Stanley Cup, his 11th, the most by a player in NHL history.

Richard beat the Blackhawks' Tony Esposito for the game-tying and game-winning (below) goals in Game 7 of the 1971 finals, earning Montreal its fifth Cup in seven years.

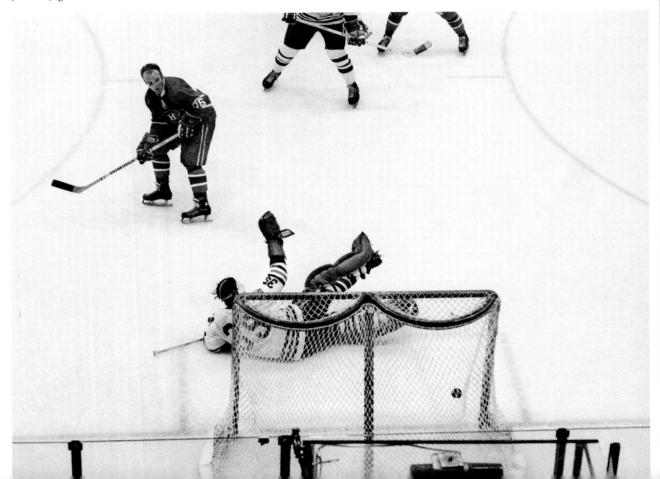

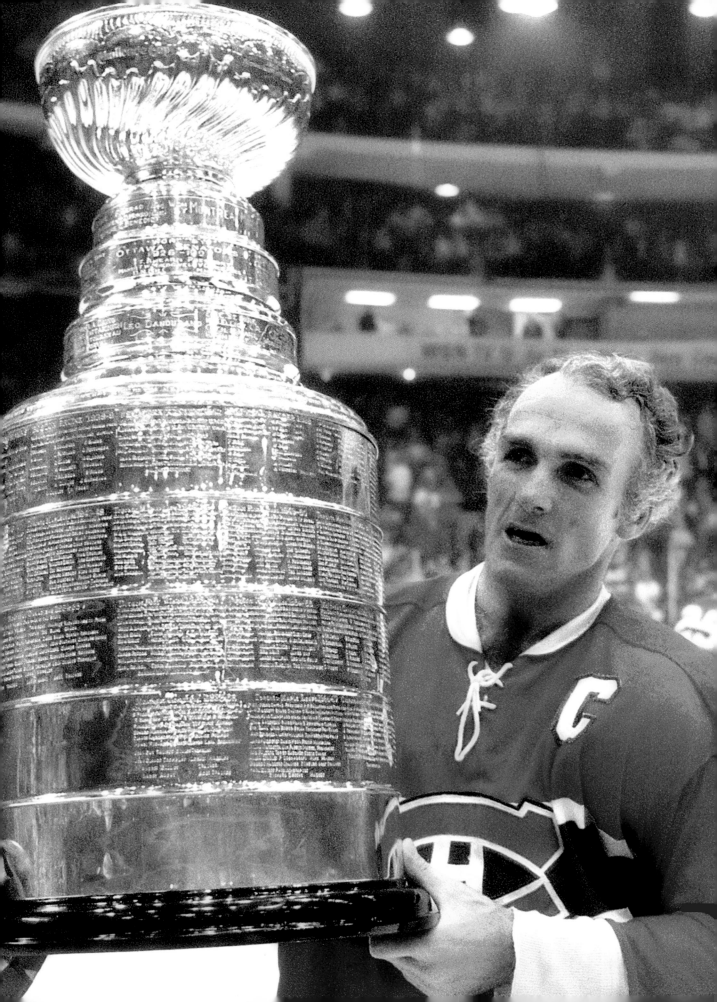

Nicknamed the Roadrunner for his speed, winger Yvan Cournoyer scored 428 goals in 16 seasons in Montreal.

Hard-hitting Robinson helped the Canadiens end a two-year Cup drought in the 1976 finals against Philadelphia.

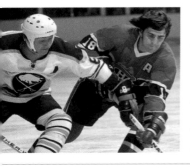

Along with Robinson and Guy Lapointe, Serge Savard (left) formed the team's Big Three defensemen, while 6' 5" forward Pete Mahovlich (below) played big for the 1971, '73, '76 and '77 title teams.

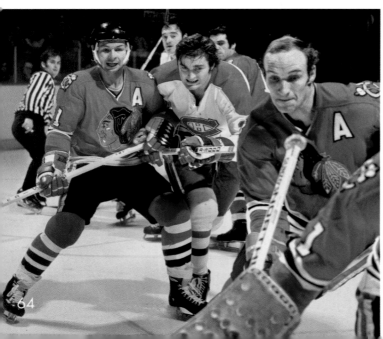

The winningest coach in NHL history, Scotty Bowman won five Stanley Cups in Montreal,
including four straight from 1976 through '79 and at least 45 games in each of his eight seasons.

Bill Nyrop played just three seasons with the
Canadiens (and only four total) but retired with
three rings, including in '77 (left).

Steve Shutt set a record
for the most single-season
goals by a left wing, 60,
in 1976–77, the same
year Montreal won an
NHL-record 60 games.

Long before he became general manager of the
Canadiens, Gainey won four Selke Trophies as
the league's best defensive forward.

THE ALL-ERA TEAM

GUY LAFLEUR

RIGHT WING, 1971–85 | Few sights were more frightening for a goaltender than Montreal's number 10 bearing down on him with the puck on his stick. Lafleur scored at least 50 goals and surpassed 100 points in six straight seasons, from 1974–75 through '79–80, resulting in a franchise-record 1,246 points.

JACQUES LEMAIRE

CENTER, 1967–79 | One of a handful of men to score the golden goal in two Stanley Cup finals, Lemaire was as consistent as he was clutch, scoring at least 20 goals in his 12 NHL seasons. He played on eight Cup champions with the Canadiens and, following his retirement, was the club's assistant general manager for two more.

BOB GAINEY

LEFT WING, 1973–89 | The first and most frequent winner of the Selke Trophy, Gainey was selected as the NHL's finest defensive forward for four consecutive seasons beginning with 1977–78. One of hockey's most respected players, Gainey was deemed the world's best all-around player by legendary Soviet coach Viktor Tikhonov.

SERGE SAVARD

DEFENSEMAN, 1966–81 | Not the most glamorous member of the Canadiens' dynasty, Savard was among the most indispensable, providing a strong defensive presence for eight championship squads. The first defenseman to win the Conn Smythe Trophy, the Senator was one of the game's true warriors, repeatedly giving up his body for the good of the team.

LARRY ROBINSON

DEFENSEMAN, 1972–89 | The MVP of the 1978 Stanley Cup playoffs, Robinson was a mainstay in the postseason, setting playoff records for consecutive games and total games, 203 of which came with Les Habs. Despite playing on the back line, Robinson ranks third alltime in playoff scoring for Montreal, with 134 career points.

KEN DRYDEN

GOALTENDER, 1970–73, '74–79 | Although he played just seven full seasons, Dryden won the Vézina Trophy five times and is the only player ever to win his sport's postseason MVP award before winning the award for top rookie. His .758 lifetime winning percentage is the highest in league history for a goalie with a minimum of 100 games.

With Dryden in the net, Montreal closed out the '70s by beating the Rangers for the Cup.

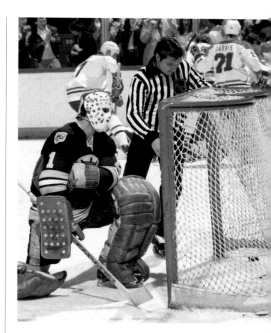

The Canadiens celebrated after an overtime victory over Boston in the storied Game 7 of the '79 playoffs.

Doug Jarvis's iron-man streak of playing in an NHL-record 964 consecutive games began with Montreal.

THE 1980s

The Canadiens were the kings of the NHL for the second time in eight seasons after defeating Los Angeles in 1993.

AND 1990s

THE KING OF THE CREASE

BY E.M. SWIFT

A SMALL GESTURE, TO BE SURE, BUT ONE as debilitating under the circumstances as the most thunderous bodycheck. Montreal Canadiens goaltender Patrick Roy merely looked at his opponent and winked. ¶ What had he been thinking? Deep into overtime in Game 4 of the Stanley Cup finals on June 7, with the Los Angeles Kings forwards literally knocking at his goalmouth, Roy stoned Luc Robitaille and froze the puck. Then, impishly, he glanced at the Kings' Tomas Sandstrom and flicked his left eyelash, like some kid in a street hockey game. This amused, unharried wink was surely one of the most memorable in hockey history. What did this outrageous gesture mean?

That Roy was cocky? That he was loose? That the puck looked as big to him as a manhole cover? That the snakebitten Kings, who had already suffered two straight backbreaking overtime losses to the Canadiens and were about to suffer their third, could play till Sunset Boulevard froze over and never poke the puck past Roy in OT?

Four days later, while riding in the backseat of a white stretch limousine in Montreal, under police escort to a Canadiens victory parade that was not about to begin without him, the 27-year-old Roy pondered that question. He could not recall ever before having winked at an opponent. Certainly not in overtime of the Stanley Cup finals. "Always Sandstrom is in my crease, bothering me, hitting at me when I have the puck," Roy said. "When I made the save on Robitaille, Sandstrom hit me. So I winked. I wanted to show him I'd be tough. That I was in control."

In control? Is that what you call Roy's remarkable 10 straight overtime wins in the 1993 playoffs, a record the Canadiens set during their run to their 24th Stanley Cup? How about invincible? Impenetrable? Or, as one fan's banner in the Montreal Forum had it, INC-ROY-HAB-LE?

After the Canadiens opened the playoffs with a loss—in OT to the Quebec Nordiques in a game in which Roy was later criticized for having let in a soft goal in the final minute to force the extra session—Roy simply closed the door when games were on the line. For the remainder of the postseason Montreal went 12–0 in one-goal games. In the 10 overtime wins Roy played 96 minutes and 39 seconds of sudden-death hockey

JOHN BIEVER

The 11-time All-Star set NHL career records for regular-season and playoff wins during a Hall of Fame career from 1985 through 2003. | *Photograph by* DAVID E. KLUTHO

without yielding a goal, the equivalent of more than a game and a half. During those extra sessions he kicked out 65 shots.

With a 16–4 record and a 2.13 goals-against average in the playoffs, Roy atoned for what had been, for him, a mediocre regular season under first-year coach Jacques Demers, who had introduced Montreal to a more wide-open style than the Canadiens had played in recent years. "The one thing as a coach I'll take credit for," said Demers after the playoffs, "is I stood with Patrick. I was not going to let him get down on himself after he gave up a soft goal against Quebec. He was just outstanding, sensational."

It wasn't the first time that Roy had put rings on the fingers of his Montreal teammates. In 1985–86, his rookie season, he also led the Canadiens to the Stanley Cup, and he won the Conn Smythe Trophy as MVP of the playoffs. But this Cup is sweeter to him than his first one was for a number of good reasons—none of which was better than the six-pound, nine-ounce daughter named Jana that Roy helped his wife, Michele, deliver on the morning after the Canadiens lost Game 1 of the finals in Montreal.

Sudden death. Sudden life. Jana's name is a cross between Jeanne, Michele's grandmother, and Anna, Patrick's grand-mother. Anna Peacock was a big-time Canadiens fan, unlike the Roys, who cheered for the hometown Quebec Nordiques of the WHA. Anna's favorite Montreal player was goalie Ken Dryden. She would listen to the games on the radio while she was feeding young Patrick his dinner.

Like Dryden, Roy was sensational in the playoffs as a rookie, leading the Canadiens to the Cup with a stunning 1.92 goals-against average.

Unlike Dryden, however, Roy stopped getting his name on the Stanley Cup after his rookie season. He was still a dominant player, winning three Vézina Trophies as the NHL's best goalie and getting named to the league's first or second All-Star team five times in the next six years. But a perception remained among Montreal fans that despite his superb statistics, Roy gave up soft goals in big games, often when his team could least afford it.

Certainly that was the rap on Roy in the '92 playoffs, when the Canadiens were ignominiously swept by the Boston Bruins in the second round. "He didn't have a good playoff last year," says Montreal general manager Serge Savard, "but he wasn't the reason we lost. It was a real team effort."

Nonetheless, Roy, the Canadiens' best player, served as a lightning rod for the criticisms of frustrated Montrealers, who, since '44, had not gone more than seven years without their team winning the Stanley Cup. And '93 brought

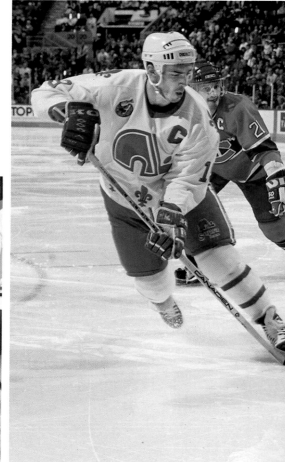

The rookie got a well-deserved rest (left) during Montreal's run to the Cup in '86. His career endured some ups and downs, but in '93 Roy stuffed Joe Sakic and the Nordiques before winning his second Stanley Cup trophy (far right) the same week his daughter Jana was born.

another seven-year itch. The once-adoring locals were starting to smell Roy's blood.

"Pat's struggles this year were new to him," says forward Kirk Muller, who, after Roy, was the most valuable Canadien in the playoffs. "Obviously people in Montreal expect a lot from him, and he can't really have a bad game—ever. But I think the struggle made him better."

When the Canadiens dropped the first two games to Quebec in the Adams Division semifinals, Demers resisted calls to start backup André Racicot in Game 3 and stayed true to a preseason promise that he would stand behind Roy all season. Ever superstitious, Roy figured it was time to change his luck. He switched the order in which he skated around the face-off circles before warming up, a ritual he had faithfully followed for seven years. When the Nordiques practiced at the Montreal Forum, he watched them from the same seat—B-7. (After Jana was born, Roy sat in J-2 in Los Angeles, in honor of her June 2 birth date.)

Presto, change-o, the Canadiens, and Roy, reeled off a record-tying 11 consecutive playoff wins. Seven of them came in overtime, including two marathon victories over the New York Islanders, who saw Roy thwart both Benoit Hogue and Pierre Turgeon on breakaways in consecutive OT games.

As the playoffs progressed, it seemed as if the Canadiens actually played for overtime, repeatedly dumping the puck in the last 10 minutes of the third period and then turning their offense loose in the extra frame. "We didn't mind going into overtime," says Roy. "I knew my teammates were going to score goals if I gave them some time. My concentration was at such a high level. My mind was right there. I felt fresh, like I could stop everything."

Fresh? Every other new father who has been through natural childbirth feels like going home and sleeping for 40 days. Here was Roy, at the end of the longest hockey season on record, shuttling between Los Angeles and Montreal, cities 2,500 miles apart, in the Stanley Cup finals, saying how wonderfully rested he felt. Winking at the opposition to prove it. Tired, Tomas? Not me.

His presence in goal seemed to sap the energy from the Kings as much as it buoyed the Canadiens, who played better and better as the finals progressed. "When Patrick Roy makes a promise, he keeps it," said Montreal forward Mike Keane after the Canadiens, in a bit of historical justice, took home the 100th Stanley Cup with a 4–1 win at home in Game 5. "He isn't an outspoken guy, but he said he was going to shut the door tonight, and he did."

In the wink of an eye. □

From SPORTS ILLUSTRATED, *June 21, 1993*

A FITTING FINALE

Bidding adieu to the Forum after winning two more Stanley Cup titles

The ghosts of the Forum were watching from the rafters on March 11, 1996, from the opening face-off (left) through the Canadiens' 4–1 win over the Stars in the 2,636th and final game in the arena.

Pierre Turgeon led teammates in a torch procession (right) before the lights went out for the final time at the Forum.

The last game at the Forum brought many Montreal stars back to the arena, including, from left, former Canadien (and then Dallas Star) Carbonneau, Guy Lafleur, Jean Béliveau, Maurice Richard and Turgeon.

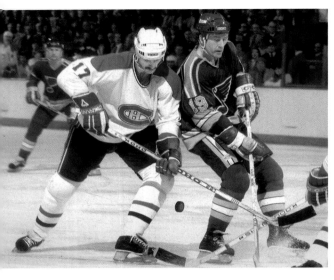

Rod Langway (17) had the look of a future Norris Trophy winner ('83, '84) as a young Canadien.

Naslund, Montreal's first European import (breaking free against the Flyers), and Carbonneau (facing off against Mario Lemieux) took the Canadiens to the brink of the '89 Cup.

Defenseman Rick Green (5) blocked a shot by Calgary's Hakan Loob in the '86 Stanley Cup finals, won by Montreal in five games.

CLOCKWISE, FROM RIGHT: DAVID BIER; DAVID E. KLUTHO (2); TONY TRIOLO

THE ALL-ERA TEAM

STÉPHANE RICHER

RIGHT WING, 1984-91, '96-98 | Using a deadly slap shot, Richer became one of the most prolific goal scorers in team history, connecting 225 times in 490 games. He scored 50 goals in 1987–88 and topped that number by one in '89–90, to become only the second Canadien, after Guy Lafleur, to score 50 or more goals in two seasons.

GUY CARBONNEAU

CENTER, 1980-81, '82-94 | Although he never scored more than 26 goals in a season, Carbonneau was most valuable to Les Habs on defense, winning the Selke Trophy three times. One of the most popular players in team history, he served as captain for five seasons. In '06 he became the 28th coach in franchise history.

MATS NASLUND

LEFT WING, 1982-90 | The first European to suit up for Le Bleu-Blanc-Rouge, Naslund was a skilled playmaker who set an NHL record for assists by a left wing in 1985–86. Le Petit Viking also scored 43 goals that season, and his 110 points remains the last time a Canadiens player reached the century mark in scoring.

LARRY ROBINSON

DEFENSEMAN, 1972-89 | With his 6' 4" frame, and flowing curly hair, Big Bird patrolled the Montreal blue line for 17 seasons, six of which ended with the Canadiens hoisting the Stanley Cup. He's the alltime franchise leader among defensemen in games played (1,202), goals (197), assists (686), points (883) and plus/minus (+700).

CHRIS CHELIOS

DEFENSEMAN, 1983-90 | No Montreal defenseman was a better offensive weapon than the hard-hitting Chelios, who averaged 0.77 of a point in 402 games with the Canadiens. In just seven seasons as a Hab, Chelios nearly did it all, winning the Stanley Cup, a Norris Trophy and finishing second to a young Mario Lemieux for the Calder Trophy.

PATRICK ROY

GOALTENDER, 1985-96 | Saint Patrick made an immediate impact on the NHL as he led the Canadiens on a magical run to the Stanley Cup and won the Conn Smythe Trophy as a 20-year-old rookie in 1986. After winning the Vézina Trophy in '89 and '90, Roy again led the Canadiens to hockey's ultimate prize in '93 while winning a second Conn Smythe.

When he wasn't toppling Kings, John LeClair (17) had two OT goals to help start the 24th Cup parade.

Referees penalized the Kings because of Marty McSorley's illegally curved stick (above), and Éric Desjardins took advantage, blasting the winning goal past Kelly Hrudey (below) in Game 2 of the '93 Stanley Cup finals.

THE 2000s

Tomas Plekanec (here scoring
against the Bruins in the '08
playoffs) is part of the quest for
the first Cup of the second century.

AND BEYOND 100

THE NEW BREED

BY BRIAN CAZENEUVE

CONSIDER SAKU KOIVU AND HIS TEAM-mates to be the keepers of the culture. Even today, long after the NHL's cozy six-team format has given way to a 30-team scramble, and fans are supposed to believe that Dallas and Tampa and North Caro-lina are hockey hotbeds because their young teams have fashioned a Stanley Cup, the NHL's flagship franchise is as relevant as ever. "You kind of measure the game by what the Canadiens do," says Koivu, Montreal's captain. "That is one thing about the game that will never really change, no matter who puts on the jersey or which year it is."

This year, of course, the relevance is heightened along with the excitement, not least because the NHL took the notable step of awarding the city both the All-Star Game in January and the entry draft in June. This year the storied franchise is tipping its cap and raising its sticks. Thanks to the shrewd foresight of general manager Bob Gainey—who began his five-year rebuild-ing program when he took over five years ago—it is a team with a bright future. And today, with a 16-year Cupless drought, the longest in franchise history, the pressure to win a title to match the anniversary's pageantry is acute.

"You can't get so caught up in the celebrations that you lose sight of the goals we have," says Koivu.

Those goals came into clear, close-up view with Montreal's Eastern Conference–best 104-point season in 2007–08, a performance the team followed by winning its first playoff round of the postlock-out era. The modern version of the Flying Frenchmen scored 257 goals for the year, one shy of league leader Ottawa. Swift and skilled, Les Habs led the league in goals on the road (130) and on the power play (90), while allowing a league-low three shorthanded scores. Right wing Alexei Kovalev, now 35, served notice that he is still a lethal threat, scoring 35 goals, including a career-high 17 with the man advantage. Center Tomas Plekanec, 26, added 29 goals, and wingers Chris Hig-gins, 25, and Andrei Kostitsyn, 23, had 27 and 26 goals, respectively. The team possessed an offensive swag-ger not seen since the days when Jacques Lemaire left drop passes for Guy Lafleur, and the resurgence was overseen, ironically, by Gainey and coach Guy Carbon-neau, both of whom were once among the game's most imposing defensive forwards.

In leading the Canadiens' revival last season, Koivu became the second-longest-tenured captain in team history. | *Photograph by* ELIOT J. SCHECHTER/NHLI/GETTY IMAGES

Gainey added more offense for this year's team, giving up draft picks to acquire Robert Lang from Chicago and Quebec-born Alex Tanguay from Calgary. Gainey also signed Georges Laraque, the league's reigning heavyweight champ and a Montreal native, to a three-year, $4.5 million contract. "It's a dream come true for me to come home again," says Laraque, a popular teammate everywhere he plays, whose signing signaled a departure from previous assertions by Gainey and Carbonneau that the team did not need an enforcer. The Canadiens were outmuscled during the postseason, both in their seven-game triumph over the Boston Bruins and in their five-game loss to the Philadelphia Flyers. Carbonneau, who didn't fight much but always played bigger than his size, emphasized a sort of team toughness, a catchphrase that will be much easier to put into practice now that Laraque has his teammates' backs.

Toughness, naturally, can also be measured in other ways: Top-pair defenseman Mike Komisarek is a fearless shot blocker (he led the NHL with 277 in 2007–08), and fellow blueliner Roman Hamrlik (187, fourth in the league) shows similar mettle. The pairing of Komisarek with reliable two-way backliner Andrei Markov has become one of the more effective tandems in the league.

Les Habs feel that they have found their goalie of the present and future, though at 21, Carey Price, the fifth overall pick in the 2005 draft, must show he is steeled enough to produce under the postseason microscope. Last season Price led rookie goalies in wins (24) and save percentage (.920) and had three shutouts but then gave up some careless goals during the playoffs. Carbonneau gambled with his young charge's confidence by replacing Price with Jaroslav Halek in Game 4 against Philadelphia. "I understand the decision," Price said then, "but obviously this is when you want to be in there most. This is when you want the guys in the room to be able to rely on you."

For more than a decade the Canadiens have relied on Koivu to be the team's driving force, much as they once relied on leaders like Maurice Richard or Jean Béliveau. After being taken by Montreal with the No. 21 pick in the 1993 draft, Koivu played a season in his native Finland, where he was named national player of the year, before coming to Montreal in '95 at age 20. Generously listed at 5' 10", 187 pounds, the center was an instant spark plug: fast, shifty, clever and deceptively strong on the puck. If he sometimes held on to it too long, he rarely turned it over, and his elusiveness made him one of the game's best at drawing penalties. His pluck and determination grew to define the new Canadiens almost as clearly as Guy Lafleur symbolized the Flying Frenchmen.

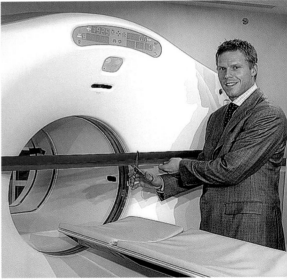

Since his battle with cancer began in 2001 (right), Koivu has been a benefactor to Montreal general hospital (above) where he was treated. These days opponents like the Devils, Rangers, Flyers and rival Maple Leafs know firsthand why the dangerous center remains such a fan favorite.

On Sept. 30, 1999, Koivu became the team's 27th captain, the first European player to be so honored. He now has the team's second-longest tenure of captaincy after Béliveau, who wore the C from 1961–62 through 1970–71.

The drive of a man who always played—and still plays—larger than his size was tested in September 2001. Koivu was traveling back from Helsinki to join the Canadiens in training camp when he began vomiting and felt severe stomach pains and headaches. Upon being examined in Montreal, Koivu, then 26, learned he was suffering from non-Hodgkin's lymphoma. The captain began undergoing chemotherapy treatments, which lasted seven months. He was soon consulting with Mario Lemieux about how to fight the disease and endure the recovery, and how to overcome loss of weight, hair and overall strength. The illness knocked Koivu out for nearly the entire season, but, stirringly, he returned for the team's next-to-last home game in April. He received an eight-minute standing ovation. That night's opponent, the Senators, banged their sticks on the ice too.

In the 2002 playoffs Koivu helped propel the Canadiens over the Bruins, and that summer he won the NHL's Bill Masterton Trophy for dedication to the game. The following season he scored a career-high 71 points.

That battle was hardly his last test. In 2006 Koivu was nearly blinded after being struck in the left eye by the stick of Carolina's Justin Williams. After surgery to reattach his retina, Koivu still suffers from some lost peripheral vision. Nonetheless, he contributed 40 assists and 16 goals last season, and delivered nine points in seven playoff games.

At 34 and in the final year of a three-year contract, Koivu remains vital to the Canadiens, who in all have eight players—Komisarek and Kovalev among them—in line to become unrestricted free agents at the end of the season. Yet the team has a strong nucleus in place and enough young talent to foster a long-absent optimism in Montreal. No matter that the Canadiens have not been to the conference finals since their Cup run of 1993. No matter that winning now, in the bloated parity-defined league, is much harder than in Les Habs' heyday. No matter the crimp that the salary cap puts on designs to keep star players for many years. "Montreal fans won't accept excuses," says Gainey. "They know the number of Stanley Cups that have been won here, and they anticipate another."

This is a franchise with many milestones in its past and many others within its reach—the Canadiens' 20th regular-season win this season will be its 3,000th in history. A 25th championship, of course, is the milestone that matters most. □

THE NEXT GENERATION

Young stars and tested veterans are poised to bring glory back to Montreal

A rejuvenated Alexei Kovalev (27) had 84 points in 2007–08, the second-highest total of his career. Drafted by the Canadiens in '94, Théodore (right) won the Vézina and Hart trophies in '02.

Right wing Ryder (73) scored 99 regular-season and three playoff goals in four seasons with the Canadiens.

With help from a Ken Dryden look-alike, Higgins (second from right) celebrated his goal against the Panthers on Feb. 13, 2008.

THE ALL-ERA TEAM

MICHAEL RYDER

RIGHT WING, 2003–08 | In his four Montreal seasons Ryder has 207 points, and his 99 goals rank first on the team during that time. At his best on the power play, Ryder was the first player in team history to score 10 or more man-advantage goals in each of his first three seasons.

SAKU KOIVU

CENTER, 1995–PRESENT | The first European-born captain of the Canadiens is the current team leader in goals (175), assists (416) and points (591). After missing 79 regular season games with non-Hodgkin's lymphoma in 2001–02, Koivu played all 12 games for Les Habs in the postseason, tying for the team lead in scoring with 10 points and earning the Bill Masterton Trophy for perseverance.

CHRISTOPHER HIGGINS

LEFT WING, 2003–PRESENT | Splitting time between the left side and center, the former Yale star and first-round draft pick has scored 20 or more goals in every one of his full pro seasons, setting career highs in goals (27) and points (52) in 2007–08.

PATRICE BRISEBOIS

DEFENSEMAN, 1990–2004, '07–PRESENT | Now in his second tour with Montreal, Brisebois ranks in the top six all time among Canadiens defensemen in games played, shots, goals, assists and points. He's been a power-play mainstay, scoring 37 goals with the man advantage, third most for Les Habs since the stat became official four decades ago.

ANDREI MARKOV

DEFENSEMAN, 2000–PRESENT | Montreal's current iron man entered the 2008–09 season having played in 128 straight games. He led the squad in time on the ice the past two seasons, averaging nearly 25 minutes per outing. Last season he tied for the league lead in power-play goals by a defenseman and was named a starter for the All-Star Game.

JOSÉ THÉODORE

GOALTENDER, 1995–2006 | In parts of nine seasons Théodore won 141 games for Montreal, including 23 shutouts, which ranks him seventh all time in franchise history in both categories. His best season was 2001–02 when he won both the Vézina and Hart trophies.

Stats through the 2007–08 season

The 25-year-old Higgins, battling the Leafs' Mats Sundin, has helped provide some offensive swagger.

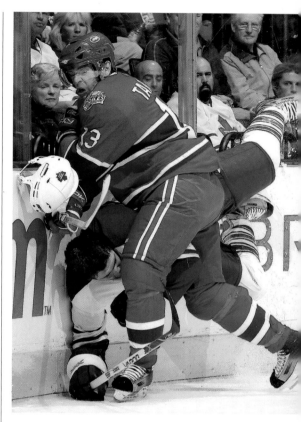

Forward Alex Tanguay, who won the Cup with Colorado in '01, joined the Canadiens this season.

Fan favorite Brisebois returned to Montreal in '07 and is now fifth on the Canadiens' alltime list for games played by a defenseman.

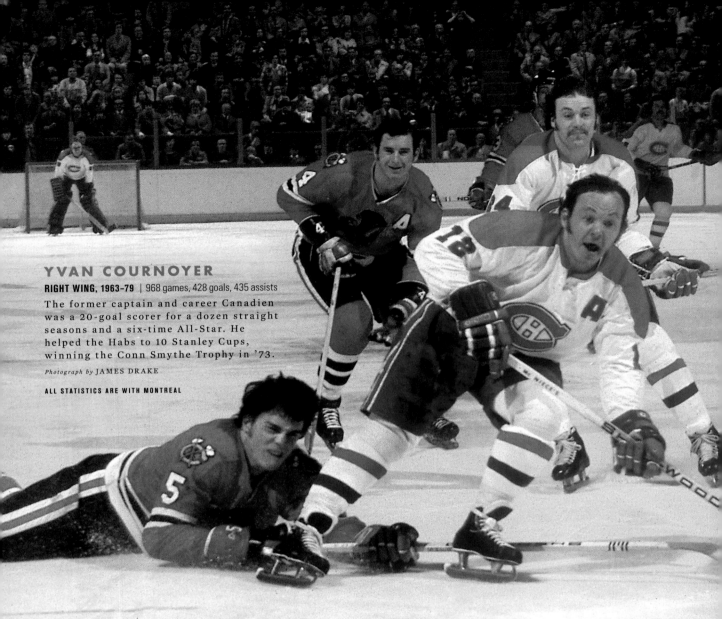

YVAN COURNOYER
RIGHT WING, 1963–79 | 968 games, 428 goals, 435 assists

The former captain and career Canadien was a 20-goal scorer for a dozen straight seasons and a six-time All-Star. He helped the Habs to 10 Stanley Cups, winning the Conn Smythe Trophy in '73.

Photograph by JAMES DRAKE

ALL STATISTICS ARE WITH MONTREAL

GREA
CANADIENS

COMPILED BY DAVID SABINO

100

TEST OF ALL TIME

HOWIE MORENZ

CENTER, 1923–34, '36–37 | 460 games, 257 goals, 160 assists

When Morenz (left) first signed with Montreal, he sent a letter to Canadiens owner Leo Dandurand saying he wasn't good enough. He then went on to become a three-time MVP, the league's onetime career goals leader and a Hockey Hall of Famer.

AURÈLE JOLIAT

LEFT WING, 1922–38 | 644 games, 270 goals, 190 assists

The former Ottawa Rough Riders football player stood a mere 5' 6" and weighed 135 pounds, but he was durable, leading the league in games played five times. He was chosen for the Hall of Fame after netting at least 10 goals in 15 straight seasons.

Photograph by IHA/ICON SMI

THE ALLTIME TEAM

RIGHT WINGS

MAURICE RICHARD | 1942-60
The Rocket remains Montreal's goals leader (544) nearly five decades after his last game.

GUY LAFLEUR | 1971-85
The top scorer in team history was drafted with a pick acquired from the Oakland Seals.

BERNIE GEOFFRION | 1950-64
In '60–61 Boom Boom joined Richard as the second NHLer to reach 50 goals in a season.

YVAN COURNOYER | 1963-79
The Roadrunner was on Stanley Cup championship teams in 10 of his 16 seasons.

CENTERS

JEAN BÉLIVEAU | 1950-51, '52-71
His 10 seasons as Canadiens captain (1961–71) is the longest tenure in team history.

HOWIE MORENZ | 1923-34, '36-37
Pro hockey's first superstar died from complications stemming from an on-ice leg injury.

HENRI RICHARD | 1955-75
Legend is that the Pocket Rocket went to Habs camp simply to humor his brother Maurice.

ELMER LACH | 1940-54
Lach was league MVP the season his linemate Maurice Richard had 50 goals in 50 games.

LEFT WINGS

DICKIE MOORE | 1951-63
The two-time Art Ross Trophy winner set the league record with 96 points in '58–59.

JOE MALONE | 1917-19, '22-24
Phantom Joe scored 44 goals in just 20 games during the Habs' first season in the NHL.

AURÈLE JOLIAT | 1922-38
The Mighty Atom earned the honor of having his number 4 retired for him and Béliveau.

BOB GAINEY | 1973-89
Gainey won the Selke Trophy as top defensive forward in each of the award's first four years.

DEFENSEMEN

DOUG HARVEY | 1947-61
The Hall of Famer honed his stickhandling and passing skills as a young center.

LARRY ROBINSON | 1972-89
Big Bird had a career plus-minus rating of +700 during his 17 seasons with the Canadiens.

SERGE SAVARD | 1966-81
The shot blocker extraordinaire scored four goals in the 1969 Stanley Cup playoffs.

GUY LAPOINTE | 1968-82
Lapointe's 28 goals in 1974–75 are the most ever scored by a Montreal defenseman.

TOM JOHNSON | 1947-48, '49-63
His penalty-killing skills were vital in Montreal's five consecutive Stanley Cups ('56–60).

JACQUES LAPERRIÈRE | 1962-74
The rock-steady Hall of Fame point man left the scoring and glamour to others.

J.C. TREMBLAY | 1959-72
His combined 21 points were second most for the Habs during the '65 and '66 playoffs.

GOALTENDERS

JACQUES PLANTE | 1952-63
Six of Plante's seven career Vézina Trophies came during his tenure with the Canadiens.

PATRICK ROY | 1984-96
Roy won the Vézina and was also named to the All-Star first team in '89, '90 and '92.

KEN DRYDEN | 1970-73, '74-79
His .758 winning percentage (258-57-74) is the NHL record for goaltenders.

GEORGES VÉZINA | 1910-26
One of the dozen original members of the Hockey Hall of Fame, he was inducted in 1945.

COACHES

HECTOR (TOE) BLAKE | 1955-68
The Habs won the Cup in his first five seasons and in eight of his 13 behind the bench.

DICK IRVIN | 1940-55
Irvin built the foundation of the post–World War II Canadiens dynasty.

SCOTTY BOWMAN | 1971-79
The Montreal native guided his hometown team to the title in five of his eight seasons.

LARRY ROBINSON

DEFENSEMAN, 1972–89 | 1,202 games, 197 goals, 686 assists

No Montreal defenseman played in more games or scored more points than Robinson (far left), who was a member of six Stanley Cup winners. He won the Norris Trophy for being the league's outstanding defenseman in '77 and '80.

GUY LAPOINTE

DEFENSEMAN, 1968–82 | 777 games, 166 goals, 406 assists

The quarterback on the point for the deadly Canadiens power play of the 1970s, Lapointe (far right) was part of the best troikas of defensemen—with Robinson and Serge Savard—ever assembled on one club.

Photograph by CO RENTMEESTER

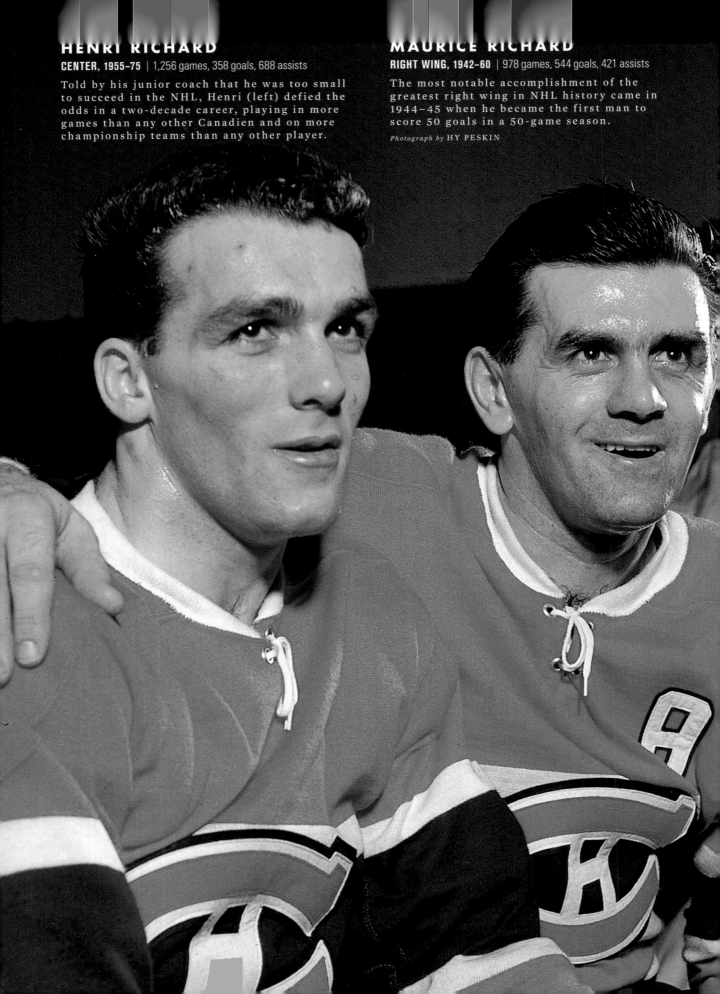

HENRI RICHARD

CENTER, 1955–75 | 1,256 games, 358 goals, 688 assists

Told by his junior coach that he was too small to succeed in the NHL, Henri (left) defied the odds in a two-decade career, playing in more games than any other Canadien and on more championship teams than any other player.

MAURICE RICHARD

RIGHT WING, 1942–60 | 978 games, 544 goals, 421 assists

The most notable accomplishment of the greatest right wing in NHL history came in 1944–45 when he became the first man to score 50 goals in a 50-game season.

Photograph by HY PESKIN

JEAN BÉLIVEAU

CENTER, 1950-51, '52-71 | 1,125 games, 507 goals, 712 assists

Béliveau initially resisted playing for Montreal, which owned his pro rights, because he was paid more in the Quebec Senior Hockey League. To oblige him to play for them, the Habs bought the league.

Photograph by FRANK PRAZAK/HOCKEY HALL OF FAME

JACQUES PLANTE

GOALTENDER, 1952–63 | 556 games,
312-134-108 record, 58 shutouts

The first NHL goalie to wear
a mask in a game, Plante is
the alltime franchise leader
in wins and games played
in goal. He led Montreal to
six Stanley Cups, including
10 postseason shutouts.

Photograph by JOHN G. ZIMMERMAN

PATRICK ROY

GOALTENDER, 1984-96 | 551 games, 289-175-66 record, 29 shutouts

As a rookie, Saint Patrick backstopped his team to 15 playoff wins and its first Stanley Cup in seven years—which at the time equaled the second-longest drought in franchise history.

Photograph by BILL BALLENBERG

JACQUES LAPERRIÈRE

DEFENSEMAN, 1962–74 | 691 games, 40 goals, 242 assists

The epitome of a defensive stopper, the '64 Calder Trophy recipient was the first rookie after World War II to be named to the NHL All-Star team. He'd go on to win the Norris Trophy as the league's top defenseman in '66.

Photograph by FRANK PRAZAK/HOCKEY HALL OF FAME

ELMER LACH

CENTER, 1940–54 | 664 games, 215 goals, 408 assists

The center on the famous Punch Line of the 1940s with Rocket Richard and Toe Blake, Lach was a creative playmaker who led the NHL in assists three times and placed in the top five four more.

Photograph by FRANK PRAZAK/ HOCKEY HALL OF FAME

DOUG HARVEY

DEFENSEMAN, 1947–61 | 890 games, 76 goals, 371 assists

The World War II Navy gunboat veteran played the blue line as deliberately as anyone who has ever laced up skates, resulting in seven Norris Trophies and six Stanley Cups.

Photograph by ARCHIVE PHOTOS/ GETTY IMAGES

GUY LAFLEUR

RIGHT WING, 1971–85 | 961 games, 518 goals, 728 assists

The famous number 10 is the Canadiens'
career leader in assists and points. For
three straight seasons he was presented
with the Lester B. Pearson Award by his
peers as the NHL's top player.

Photograph by JOHN IACONO

LEADERS

Prime Numbers

A compendium of Montreal's top performers | COMPILED BY ELIZABETH McGARR

GOALS

544	MAURICE RICHARD	1942–60
518	GUY LAFLEUR	1971–85
507	JEAN BÉLIVEAU	1950–51, '52–71
428	YVAN COURNOYER	1963–79
408	STEVE SHUTT	1972–85
371	BERNIE GEOFFRION	1950–64
366	JACQUES LEMAIRE	1967–79
358	HENRI RICHARD	1955–75
270	AURÈLE JOLIAT	1922–38
258	MARIO TREMBLAY	1974–86

ASSISTS

728	GUY LAFLEUR	1971–85
712	JEAN BÉLIVEAU	1950–51, '52–71
688	HENRI RICHARD	1955–75
686	LARRY ROBINSON	1972–89
469	JACQUES LEMAIRE	1967–79
435	YVAN COURNOYER	1963–79
421	MAURICE RICHARD	1942–60
416	SAKU KOIVU	1995–present
408	ELMER LACH	1940–54

POINTS

1,246	GUY LAFLEUR	1971–85
1,219	JEAN BÉLIVEAU	1950–51, '52–71
1,046	HENRI RICHARD	1955–75
965	MAURICE RICHARD	1942–60
883	LARRY ROBINSON	1972–89
863	YVAN COURNOYER	1963–79
835	JACQUES LEMAIRE	1967–79
776	STEVE SHUTT	1972–85
759	BERNIE GEOFFRION	1950–64

SEASONS

20	HENRI RICHARD	1955–75
18	MAURICE RICHARD	1942–60
18	JEAN BÉLIVEAU	1950–51, '52–71
17	LARRY ROBINSON	1972–89
16	AURÈLE JOLIAT	1922–38
16	BOB GAINEY	1973–89

50-GOAL SEASONS

6	GUY LAFLEUR	1971–85
2	STÉPHANE RICHER	1984–91, '96–98
1	MAURICE RICHARD	1942–60
1	BERNIE GEOFFRION	1950–64
1	STEVE SHUTT	1972–85
1	PIERRE LAROUCHE	1977–82

100-POINT SEASONS

6	GUY LAFLEUR	1971–85
2	PETER MAHOVLICH	1969–78
1	STEVE SHUTT	1972–85
1	MATS NASLUND	1982–90

The Pocket Rocket is the franchise leader in games and seasons played.

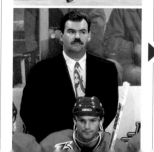

MOST POINTS SCORED IN ONE GAME

8	MAURICE RICHARD	Dec. 28, 1944
8	BERT OLMSTEAD	Jan. 9, 1954
7	NEWSY LALONDE	Jan. 11, 1919
7	JEAN BÉLIVEAU	March 7, 1959
7	YVAN COURNOYER	Feb. 15, 1975
7	STÉPHANE RICHER	Feb. 14, 1990

GAMES

1,256	HENRI RICHARD	1955–75
1,202	LARRY ROBINSON	1972–89
1,160	BOB GAINEY	1973–89
1,125	JEAN BÉLIVEAU	1950–51, '52–71
1,005	CLAUDE PROVOST	1955–70

PENALTY MINUTES

2,248	CHRIS NILAN	1979–88, 1991–92
1,367	LYLE ODELEIN	1989–96
1,341	SHAYNE CORSON	1985–92, '96–2000
1,285	MAURICE RICHARD	1942–60
1,214	JOHN FERGUSON	1963–71

GOALTENDERS, GAMES PLAYED

556	JACQUES PLANTE	1952–63
551	PATRICK ROY	1984–96
397	KEN DRYDEN	1970–73, '74–79
383	BILL DURNAN	1943–50
353	JOSÉ THÉODORE	1995–2006

GOALTENDER WINS

312	JACQUES PLANTE	1952–63
289	PATRICK ROY	1984–96
258	KEN DRYDEN	1970–73, '74–79
208	BILL DURNAN	1943–50
167	GEORGE HAINSWORTH	1926–33, '36–37
144	MICHEL LAROCQUE	1973–81

GOALTENDER SHUTOUTS

75	GEORGE HAINSWORTH	1926–33, '36–37
58	JACQUES PLANTE	1952–63
46	KEN DRYDEN	1970–73, '74–79
34	BILL DURNAN	1943–50
29	PATRICK ROY	1984–96

GOALS-AGAINST AVERAGE
(MIN. 100 GAMES PLAYED)

1.78	GEORGE HAINSWORTH	1926–33, '36–37
2.23	JACQUES PLANTE	1952–63
2.24	KEN DRYDEN	1970–73, '74–79
2.36	BILL DURNAN	1943–50
2.36	GERRY McNEIL	1947–48, '49–54, '56–57

ALLTIME COACHING VICTORIES

500	HECTOR (TOE) BLAKE	1955–68
431	DICK IRVIN	1940–55
419	SCOTTY BOWMAN	1971–79
174	PAT BURNS	1988–92
148	CECIL HART	1926–32
126	JEAN PERRON	1985–88

COVERS

HABS IN THE HEADLINES

One hundred years and 24 Cups, through the eyes of SI | COMPILED BY ADAM DUERSON

I T MAY BE HARD FOR THE FANS OF ANY OTHER NHL TEAM TO FULLY APPRECIATE THE UPS AND downs of the Montreal Canadiens' 100-year history: the four years in the '70s that Les Canadiens didn't win it all, the dire '40s when they brought home only two Cups—*mon Dieu!* For their sake, we'll stick to the good times; as these covers from SPORTS ILLUSTRATED's 54 years prove, there have been plenty of those.

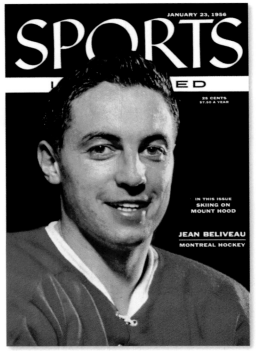

JANUARY 23, 1956
Béliveau was the portrait of a Canadien, here before the first of five straight Cup championships.

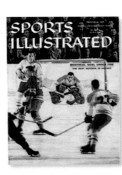

FEBRUARY 17, 1958
With Jacques in net, these Habs were hard to supplant.

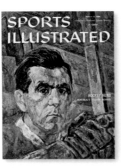

MARCH 21, 1960
The end of the line for the Rocket—and for the title run.

FEBRUARY 14, 1972
Ken Dryden laid down the law and dominated the '70s.

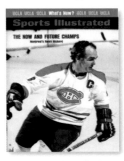

APRIL 2, 1973
The Rocket's *petit frère*, Henri, pocketed his record 11th Cup.

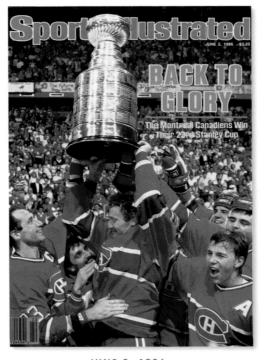

JUNE 2, 1986
One more for Big Bird. Hall of Famer Larry Robinson (center) won six Cups with Montreal.

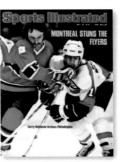

MAY 24, 1976
Robinson's D keyed the first of two straight undefeated finals.

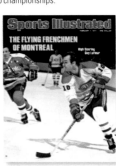

FEBRUARY 7, 1977
Lafleur's career year: He flowered in the playoffs with 26 points.

MAY 29, 1978
Tough defense helped Montreal hold off the scrappy Bruins.

NBA Finals: NOT JUST THE CHARLES & MICHAEL SHOW

Sports Illustrated

JUNE 14, 1993 $2.95 U.S./$3.95 CANADA

Très Bien, Canadiens

Montreal upends Los Angeles in the Stanley Cup

JUNE 14, 1993

Victoire! Montreal survived three overtime games and an early series deficit en route to its most recent Stanley Cup.

THE PEOPLE'S TEAM

Their service to *les habitants* of Quebec is the Canadiens' legacy | BY JEAN BÉLIVEAU *as told to Michael Farber*

AS THE MONTREAL CANADIENS CELebrate their 100th anniversary this season, some people say, "One hundred, that's only a number." Yes, it's a number. But try to keep an organization or a company together for 100 years. I read an article once that said more than three quarters of family businesses don't last three generations. The Canadiens are not a family business, but they feel like a family, and they have lasted. And I think you'll agree the Canadiens are no ordinary company.

I travel across Canada and see the number of Montreal jerseys out West and in the Maritimes and think of the great level of support this team has everywhere, not just in Quebec. In Quebec, of course, many people identify with the success of the team, the great victories over the 100 years. Because of those successes, the Canadiens have instilled a belief among the people of this province that we, too, can accomplish great things—and in the proper way.

This team's following has been passed down from generation to generation. I remember sitting in our house in Victoriaville in 1945 and listening to *Hockey Night in Canada* on the big radio as Maurice scored 50 goals in 50 games. Every backyard had its little sheet of ice, and you could be Maurice or Elmer Lach or Toe Blake or Milt Schmidt from Boston or Gordie. There's no doubt for us that Maurice was the hero, but as I got older I found myself playing center, so for me Elmer was also special. When Elmer was injured in '52, I was called up to replace him for three games and played a little bit with Elmer

Béliveau, 77, has been associated with the Canadiens' organization for 55 years.

after I signed my first contract in '53.

I'm 77 now, and I have been part of this great organization for 55 straight years. I could never imagine any association lasting that long. I'm very proud of that relationship, because no matter what has happened on the ice, the Canadiens always have tried to do things the right way—looking to the future while honoring the past. My title is ambassador, meaning I do speaking engagements and sign autographs, but I'm not one to glue myself to the team, so I mostly stand back. Things are different now; it's a different era with different players than when I played, and this is *their* time.

My time was two generations ago. Many people who come to the games today never saw me play; they compare players now with what they saw in the 1980s. I always had a lot of respect for those who preceded me. Maybe we weren't well-paid, but we earned more than the players in the '20s and '30s did. I always had a feeling those players built this franchise for us, and I have a feeling that our gang in the '50s and '60s built it for the gang of the late '70s and '80s. I think this current group of players understands that, especially with what's been going on with the 100th anniversary.

Any team means a lot to its fans, but the Canadiens create a different feeling because they are so closely tied to Montreal and the province. In 2000 the franchise started the Montreal Canadiens Children's Foundation. My own foundation, in 1993, was transferred to the Quebec Society for Disabled Children. Alex Kovalev has started Kovy's Kids for sick and underprivileged kids. The Saku Koivu Foundation raises money for cancer treatment. If everyone is doing his share, then the people benefit.

In the 100th year we have to remember that the Canadiens will always be the people's team. □

Photograph by PAUL CHIASSON/CP/AP